Deleting the State

Deleting the State

*An Argument about
Government*

AEON J. SKOBLE

OPEN COURT
Chicago and La Salle, Illinois

To order books from Open Court, call toll-free 1-800-815-2280,
or visit our website at www.opencourtbooks.com.

Open Court Publishing Company is a division of Carus Publishing Company.

Printed and bound in the United States of America.

Library of Congress Cataloging-in-Publication Data

Skoble, Aeon J.
    Deleting the state : an argument about government / Aeon J. Skoble.
      p. cm.
    Summary: "Argues that political authority is illegitimate, and in doing so explores
perennial questions in political philosophy such as the nature and extent of state
authority and political obligation, the relation of individual freedom to the collective
good, and the reconciliation of political power with personal autonomy"—Provided
by publisher.
    Includes bibliographical references and index.
    ISBN-13: 978-0-8126-9614-1 (trade paper : alk. paper)
    1. Political science—Philosophy. 2. Political obligation. 3. Authority. 4. State, The.
I. Title.
JA71.S48484 2008
320.101—dc22
                          2008004022

Contents

Acknowledgments

As Leonard Read demonstrated so succinctly, the input of many people is necessary for the accomplishment of any project, even if they do not realize they are so contributing. His example was a pencil, but it is true even in the case of something as individualistic as writing a book. I could not have produced this book in a vacuum. I am fortunate to have had the moral support, and in some cases, financial support of a pretty large cast of characters. Some of these people literally helped in the sense of contributing directly to my ability to formulate arguments. In other cases it was a help just knowing that I had their support and encouragement. I need to single out David Ramsay Steele, my editor at Open Court, for his many excellent suggestions as well as his willingness to take on this project. I am also grateful to two anonymous reviewers for their comments. I am specifically grateful for generous financial support in the form of grants from, first, the Earhart Foundation, and later, The Center for the Advancement of Research and Teaching at Bridgewater State College, where I am fortunate enough to have a position. The people I would like to thank for their help in the various forms mentioned above include, alphabetically, Randy Barnett, Don Boudreaux, Mark T. Conard, Douglas J. Den Uyl, the people at the Foundation for Economic Education, John Hasnas, Lester Hunt, the people at the Institute for Humane Studies, Jonathan Jacobs, the people at Liberty Fund, Roderick Long, Tibor Machan, James Otteson, John Pappas, my current and emeritus colleagues in the Philosophy Department at Bridgewater State College (the department than which none more congenial can be conceived), and Douglas B. Rasmussen. (If I've forgotten to mention someone, I apologize—you helped too, thanks!) I also want to express thanks and appreciation to my wife, Lisa Bahnemann, for the support she has given me. Lastly, I want to thank Lydia Skoble and Madeleine Skoble for making me care even more about the future—here's hoping they inherit a more free world.

1

Liberalism, Libertarianism, and the State

Centralized, coercive political authority—the State—is not necessary. The minimal-state version of libertarianism or classical liberalism is inconsistent in justifying state coercion, because the core concerns that prompt minimal-state libertarians to defend the state can be addressed to their satisfaction.

Many such theorists have said that political authority is undesirable, but think it is also unavoidable or necessary. Others have said that political authority *is* desirable, but the standard line in the classical liberal tradition is that coercion is a necessary evil. The basic logical schema for demonstrating the illegitimacy of political authority would be along the lines of a logician's modus ponens: If P were true, then Q would be true. P *is* true. So, Q is true.

I will argue along the following lines:

1. If it's good for people to be free, then *political* authority is illegitimate.

2. It *is* good for people to be free.

3. So, *political* authority is illegitimate.

To say that political authority is illegitimate is to invite a variety of misreadings, so let me clarify before proceeding. The distinction between political authority and other sorts of authority is one which occupies considerable portions of what follow, but for now suffice it to say that I am not advancing an argument for moral

1

subjectivism, or against the authority of scientists in their fields of expertise, or against all structural authorities such as a General or a CEO. I am speaking here only of the authority of the state, of political leaders or rulers. Also, by 'illegitimate', I do not mean to suggest that the laws we currently have were not passed in proper fashion, or that one particular government is legitimate while others are not, or that we ought all of a sudden to don black and violently attack the existing power structure. Indeed, I think (and will argue) that this last especially is a serious mistake. But my argument, if successful, will show that the state lacks *moral* justification in any *theoretical* way, and this, I claim, has ramifications for how we think about social order generally, and possible political reforms.

The second premise, that liberty is good for people, has been defended with many fine arguments over the last couple of centuries. I shall make such an argument myself, although I make no attempt to pass it off as original. I think that several thinkers have made the case far more persuasively and completely than I could, but many remain unconvinced, so it bears continual reiterating and restating. What I will offer is a version of what I think is the most persuasive case for individual liberty.

The first premise, though, is where some new thinking is called for, since even classical liberals tend to argue that the state is a necessary evil. It is the argument for this that occupies the bulk of this effort. If we start with the assumption that liberty is good, I hope to show that that entails the case against coercive political authority.

The list of perennial questions in political philosophy includes such things as the nature and extent of state authority and political obligation, the relation of individual freedom to the collective good, and the reconciliation of political power with personal autonomy. Ever since the Enlightenment, particularly since John Locke wrote about the importance of government by consent and the natural condition of individual liberty, any theory of political authority has had to take into account the concerns of those who value the freedom and autonomy of the individual. People have undoubtedly been concerned with their own freedom since before there was a theoretical vocabulary to describe these concerns, but political power was typically grounded in ways that had little to do with what we now think of pre-reflectively as individual rights. The idea that individual freedom needed to be *theoretically* incorporated into any theory of political authority is essentially a product of the Enlightenment, and even theorists who have since disparaged the role of the individual feel at least obliged to explain why. But despite the attention paid to the conception of individual freedom since the Enlightenment, questions still remain about reconciling the apparent conflict between the power of the state and the autonomy of the individual human being.

In the liberal tradition, there is no natural *being* called 'a state'. The state is a social institution. Indeed, one of the hallmarks of the liberal tradition is the insistence on the artificiality of the state. This stands in contrast to, for instance, the old monarchist conception that the sovereign embodies the nation, that the king of Spain *is* Spain, or the fascist notion (also adopted by the National Socialists) that the state is a racial organism (see, for instance, Hitler 1943, 150). Hitler, and before him Mussolini, derive this from Hegel, who says that the state is "the actuality of the ethical idea" and that "the state has the supreme right against the individual, whose supreme duty is to be a member of the State" (cited in Shirer 1959, 98). To the liberal tradition, this is exactly backwards, as the state's power must derive from the people and be limited in scope to protect the rights of the people (although there is of course disagreement within liberalism about how to specify these conditions). The power of the state is thus the power of an individual or group of individuals who wield power under the rubric of authority that is called 'the state'. This typically entails a legitimacy respected by others; that is, the fact that the state has power over people is accepted by those people for whatever reason. But therein lies a difficulty. Is the reason offered a coherent one? Is it of motivating force for the people concerned? What happens when some accept the authority and others do not? Clearly it is a matter of importance to determine the extent to which one accepts another's power over oneself. An evaluation of the basis for political authority is therefore a task facing each individual. Is there any such basis? If so, what are its limits? If not, what are the consequences? These are large questions, and my goal here is to begin with a narrower one, with an eye to using the results of the narrow inquiry to address the larger.

It is one thing to argue that the state should be strictly limited in the scope of its powers in order to preserve individual freedom; it is quite another to argue that the state is essentially incompatible with individual freedom and that therefore no state should be permitted. The first is commonly known as 'minimal state' theory, or sometimes simply libertarianism. The minimal state theory of the liberal tradition is distinguished from contemporary anarchist theory not by fundamental values, but by a connected group of concerns which are taken to justify state coercion.

While my discussion is chiefly concerned with anarchists of more recent vintage, there is a long history of anarchist thought going back over 150 years, to figures such as Gustave de Molinari, Pierre-Joseph Proudhon, Auberon Herbert, Mikhail Bakunin, Peter Kropotkin, and William Godwin. The anarchist's claim is that a lack of political authority is in some sense preferable to the presence of political authority. Proponents of such a theory would point out that the word 'anarchy' is not originally synonymous with chaos, something generally considered to be bad, although the word is often used this way. The challenge to anyone wishing to defend this view has typically been to show why a lack of political authority would not amount to chaos. Statist theory (minimal or otherwise) has it that the political authority is at least necessary (although this is often an implicit, not an explicit, premise) and can often be a positive good. Minimal-state theory is that species of classical liberal theory which holds that the state is not a positive good, and should be viewed with suspicion and severely limited in its scope. I will argue that minimal-state theorists implicitly appeal to a particular set of concerns that, despite the general presumption against the state, are taken to justify its authority.

My aim here is to isolate and examine these core worries about the threat of chaos and to test them conceptually against anarchist responses to the challenges they pose. I intend to show how certain fundamental problems in this area have been largely neglected by philosophers (in the narrow sense of members of philosophy departments), but have been addressed by theorists in fields such as economics and law, and I will interpret the philosophical significance of these arguments. In other words, I think there are arguments made by theorists from disciplines other than philosophy which may profitably be brought to bear on this very philosophical problem. I will begin with some preliminary arguments establishing the general framework for the theories I will examine. Then I will more specifically explicate the key concepts 'coercion' and 'the state', a clear understanding of which is essential if my arguments are not to be reduced to mere disagreements over definition. I will present a case for liberty in the context of exploring these. Chapters 3 and 4 represent the heart of what is original in my project. Chapter 3 isolates the central concerns that either tacitly or explicitly motivate minimal-state liberal theorists in their justification of state authority by showing the essential role these concerns play in those arguments. This will involve distinguishing different approaches to minimal-state theory in order to see how representative theorists of various approaches justify state coercion, something which they are predisposed against. I argue that, despite the fact that these theorists approach the defense of liberty with different strategies, their defenses of the minimal state against anarchist criticism are all based on a similar strategy based on shared underlying premises about the necessity of the state. Understanding the nature and origin of these underlying premises, and seeing the role they play in the various theories will enable me to frame them as a challenge to anyone wishing to argue against state authority. Chapter 4 examines various anarchist attempts to respond to this challenge and to deny the underlying justification of political authority. It is at this point that I shall supplement the philosophical investigation with a consideration of some recent work in economics, decision theory, and jurisprudence. Chapter 5 presents an extended example of how social cooperation might arise in the absence of a state. Chapter 6, by way of making some concluding observations, gives a glimpse of how this narrow inquiry can be used in larger inquiries by looking, first, at how statist systems develop and overtake non-statist systems, a concern for anyone wishing to defend anarchism, and second, at some potential difficulties in reaching common ground when engaged in disputes with proponents of different approaches to political theory. I conclude with a postscript arguing that even if it is true that the state lacks moral legitimacy, violent actions against the state are nevertheless not justified.

An important clarification: 'anarchism' is a word which needs to be divorced from its unpleasant connotations (chaos, violence, and so on) if the political theory which it signifies is to be explored. It also needs to be said that opposition to *political* authority does not entail opposition to social order of some sort, or moral theory, or specific institutional hierarchies, or the laws of logic and science. Although some who defend anarchism make these inferences, I think they are mistaken. Perhaps the word 'anarchist', then, is too misleading to be useful and should be given up in favor of a term that lacks those connotations. Some have suggested 'radical libertarianism', or 'non-monopolistic legal system' or 'polycentric law', or use the locution 'political-legal order'. I will return to this issue after the argument is concluded. For now, I ask the reader's indulgence in remembering that, connotations aside, the word denotes nothing more than opposition to rulers (archons).

It might seem as though I am only concerned with mediating an internal dispute in liberal theory, namely whether or not the authority of the state can be justified at all given the fundamental starting point of individual liberty as a value, a common ground among many schools of liberalism, including of course libertarianism. But ultimately the argument transcends that apparent parochialism, since I will argue that indeed those common premises are correct, that people *ought* to have social structures which maximize their liberty. Even among classical liberals there is likely to be dispute over the nature of liberty, and *why* it is important to have a political order that respects individual liberty, but they all agree on certain fundamentals, for example *that* it is important for the political order to respect individual liberty. This means that we can expect there to be a good deal of agreement surrounding what I claim to be an interesting disagreement, for example about our key concepts of 'state' and 'coercion'. To those who do not accept the classical liberal's claims about the primacy of liberty, I hope to persuade them that this is indeed the most beneficial framework for a social theory.

Let me begin by trying to situate the argument in terms of political philosophy generally.

Libertarians spend a good portion of their time explaining why government needs to be severely limited in its scope. This activity is frequently met with the rejoinder that the logical consequence of this view is anarchism. This is, of course, intended as a *reductio ad absurdum*. Most libertarians at this point explain that the government's only proper role is in protecting people from force and fraud, but nothing else, thus conceding the point that if the logical consequence *were* anarchism, then there would indeed be something wrong with the view. Some libertarians, however, deny the attempted *reductio*. They reply that the reasoning does lead to anarchism, but that there is nothing wrong with that. This proves that not all libertarians agree about everything. It is one thing to argue that the state should be strictly limited in the scope of its powers in order to preserve individual freedom; it is quite another to argue that the state is essentially incompatible with individual freedom and that therefore no state should be permitted.

Not all anarchists derive their views from a radical extension of the principles of libertarianism. If we look at the history of anarchist thought, we notice that the individualist anarchists represent but one of several types of anarchism. Others have attempted to derive the conclusion that no government is justified from premises more typical of socialist theory. Early anarchism was a part of the same generation of social-revolutionary movements that produced Marxism. Hence we find Pierre-Joseph Proudhon asking in 1840 "What is property?" and answering with the word "theft," not the answer one would expect to hear from a libertarian. Yet Proudhon was essentially in favor of property, in the sense of farmers owning the land they farmed. He did think that social arrangements should be based on voluntary contractual agreement. The words that theorists use often have contexts which get lost over time, and this is no exception. If we define 'property' as absentee landlordism derived from royal prerogative, then calling property theft makes a little more sense. Indeed, in the 1840s, the word 'socialism' implied *acceptance* of the market, hence the attacks on 'socialism' (as opposed to 'communism') in early Marxist writings. The differences between individualist anarchists and collectivist anarchists are sometimes difficult to ascertain with any specificity. Mikhail Bakunin advocated common ownership of the means of production, yet split with Marx over the issues of authority and liberty. In the 1890s Peter Kropotkin took up the slogan (actually coined by Louis Blanc but associated with Marx's "higher phase of communism"), "From each according to his ability, to each according to his needs," and saw the state as an agent of moral corruption. Max Stirner, on the other hand, was a radical individualist. A contemporary of Marx and Bakunin, Stirner rejected the very notion of society, advocating a loose union of egoists.

The difference seems to be this: some see anarchism as the logical result of the social nature of man, freely joining into collective, yet decentralized, associations. Others see anarchism as the extension of the priority of individual liberty. Perhaps unsurprisingly, the early American anarchists tended to be of the individualist variety. From Josiah Warren in the 1850s to Lysander Spooner and Benjamin Tucker in the 1870s and 1880s to Albert Jay Nock in the 1930s, the development of anarchism in America has been an integral part of libertarian history. The individualist ideals of these early writers formed part of an intellectual landscape where the ideas of liberty could be developed free from any neo-Hegelian notions of History's Progress.

In American libertarian thought, the problem has not been so much whether individualism or collectivism formed the basis for anarchism, but whether the priority of individual liberty could be reconciled with a minimal state, or required its absence. By calling themselves 'individualist', the American libertarians meant to differentiate themselves from their communist counterparts, but on closer analysis, we see that they are simply emphasizing the idea that individual rights are the basis for human association and a necessary component of any social cooperation. As libertarians never tire of pointing out, a society based on individual liberty and private property permits individuals to (for example) associate in communes or other collective arrangements if they wish, whereas a communist culture would not permit the variety of contractual relations common to liberal societies.

Libertarianism and Liberalism

The first step towards establishing a framework is to make some important distinctions. The liberal tradition in political philosophy is generally construed as being concerned with (to varying degrees) liberty, hence the name. This tradition is generally regarded as a product of the Enlightenment, specifically Locke's claims that individuals have 'natural' rights against the power of the sovereign, although, according to many, certain principles of liberalism have much older precedents.

For example, one common tenet of liberal thought is the idea of a 'higher law' which serves as a limit on the power of a ruler. In the *Republic*, Plato famously argues for a conception of justice that is beyond and conceptually prior to the commands of human rulers, and in the *Minos*,[1] he anticipates the natural law tradition of Aquinas (and to a lesser extent the natural rights theorists of the Enlightenment) with claims that laws themselves must conform to reality if they are to be considered valid.

> [We won't say that] law is a decision of the political community. . . . For it would not be fitting for a bad decision to be law. (*Minos* 314c)

> Whatever is not the right thing we shall deny is the binding thing. . . . It is thus unlawful [necessarily]. (317c)

For Plato, the laws were to conform to realities about the nature of human existence. For Aquinas, man-made laws could only command respect and obedience if they conformed to the law of God to serve the human good and not merely the interest of the ruler. Unjust laws "are acts of violence rather than laws; because [quot-

---

1. There is scholarly dispute as to whether the *Minos* is spurious or genuine. For present purposes, it makes no difference, as my only point in mentioning it is to highlight an important early entry in the natural law tradition later refined by Aquinas.

ing Augustine] 'a law that is not just, seems to be no law at all.' Wherefore such laws do not bind in conscience . . ." (Quest. 96, art. 4).

Nevertheless, kings continued to rule, frequently by appeal to a divine right to rule. This was the generally accepted norm which John Locke challenged in his *Two Treatises of Government*. The 'natural law' tradition of Aquinas would finally be brought to bear on real political structures in Locke's criticism of divine right theories and his defense of consent as the necessary condition of just government. Locke's conception of government by consent (eventually) made widespread the notion that individuals had a right to their own persons, from which followed a right to the products of their labor. On this understanding, persons were to be secure in their liberty and possessions from arbitrary actions of the sovereign.

"[E]very Man has a Property in his own Person. This no Body has any Right to but himself" (*Second Treatise*, Section 27). For Locke, government was rightly understood as an artifice to protect these rights. "The great and chief end therefore, of Mens . . . putting themselves under Government, is the Preservation of their Property" (Section 124), and by property Locke means "Lives, Liberties and Estates, which I call by the general Name, Property" (Section 123). The appeal of government by consent lies in this conception of self-ownership or personal freedom, which is a completely different conception of human beings from the one implicit in a theory of divine right of kings. I will not be concerned here with refuting theories of divine right of kings, although I do hope to show why another theory, that of the value of individual liberty, is one worth taking seriously. I will also be concerned to show, of course, whether classical liberalism can consistently maintain that liberty is good and that coercive authority is justified.

Liberalism since Locke has been developed in various directions,[2] but the one I am concerned with at present is the direction

---

2. Jules Coleman is correct when he opens his 1992 book *Risks and Wrongs* with the statement that "It is impossible to characterize liberalism in either a comprehensive or an uncontroversial fashion" (1). But I think he is also correct in his attempt to do so: "Sometimes liberalism is thought to identify a set of political or

known as minimal-state liberalism, which is also known as 'libertarianism' or 'classical liberalism'. Minimal-state liberalism is sometimes characterized as the theory that the only proper role of political authority is protecting the citizens from force and fraud. Two other 'popular' formulations of this idea are Thomas Jefferson's claim that the government which governs best, governs least; and John Stuart Mill's "very simple principle . . . that the sole end for which mankind are warranted, individually or collectively, in interfering with the liberty of action of any of their number is self-protection" (*On Liberty*, 68).

Being a 'liberal', then, is not a sufficiently descriptive category, for one might accept the liberal conceptions of personal freedom and autonomy, but disagree with Mill that protection against force and fraud is the "sole end" of government. One might, for example, argue that an "end" of government is ensuring "equitable distribution of resources," or some other thing. Being a 'classical liberal' (or a libertarian or a minimal-state theorist) will delineate a *sort* of liberalism, then, one whose priorities with regard to the limits of state authority place primary emphasis on liberty. Both the anarchist theorists and minimal state theorists in question will share this concern with the person's political liberty.

Anarchism and the Minimal State

If being a libertarian (as opposed to some other variety of liberal) is about what values one thinks are important, being an anarchist or a minimal-statist is a different distinction. To be an anarchist is to argue that there is no justification for political authority. (There is an etymological similarity between anarchism and atheism, but this is superficial: the atheist denies that the thing in question

---

moral *values*, for example, autonomy, equality, or neutrality. Other times liberalism is identified with concrete political *rights* . . . [such as] freedom of expression, religion, and association. Yet other times it is thought to articulate a form or family of political *justifications* or constraints on justificatory strategies, for example, the claim that political authority must be justified to those individuals against whom the coercive powers of the state are to be deployed" (Coleman 1992, 1).

exists, the anarchist recognizes the existence of governments but denies their legitimacy. To be an atheist is not merely to deny God's legitimacy or authority.) To be even a minimal statist is to argue that there is some justification for state authority. Obviously, there is room for disagreement between two statists about the bounds of political authority, and the word 'statist' is as fraught with connotations as the word 'anarchist'. Minimal-state libertarians will bristle at being called statists, since the word is often used to describe a proponent of strong, centralized authority. These labeling issues will be best dealt with *after* I have made my arguments, so again I ask the reader's indulgence temporarily. I am here using statist merely to mean anyone who thinks there some justification for a state, even a minimal, libertarian one, though I shall try to specify 'minimal-statist' when I can do so without being too inelegant.

The focus of my investigations here is the different arguments of an anarchist who is a libertarian and a minimal-state libertarian. What makes this interesting is the common ground about what sorts of considerations are relevant in political philosophy, in this case, personal freedom and autonomy. The disagreement concerns the justification or lack thereof for state authority. The question is, can *minimal-state* libertarianism be consistently maintained?

For example, Robert Nozick opens his 1974 book *Anarchy, State, and Utopia* by writing:

> Our main conclusions about the state are that a minimal state, limited to the narrow functions of protection against force, theft, fraud, enforcement of contracts, and so on, is justified; that any more extensive state will violate persons' rights not to be forced to do certain things, and is unjustified; and that the minimal state is inspiring as well as right. Two noteworthy implications are that the state may not use its coercive apparatus for the purpose of getting some citizens to aid others, or in order to prohibit activities to people for their *own* good or protection. . . . it is only coercive routes toward these goals that are excluded. (Nozick 1974, ix)

This is a commonly accepted and explicit statement of the libertarian position, that is, the position of libertarians who do support the minimal state. Of the three "main conclusions" Nozick lists, the second two are accepted by anarchist libertarians as well; it is the first that is denied. Consider for contrast the anarchist libertarian position set out by Murray Rothbard in his 1978 essay "Society Without a State":

> I define anarchist society as one where there is no legal possibility for coercive aggression against the person or property of any individual. Anarchists oppose the state because it has as its very being such aggression, namely, the expropriation of private property through taxation, the coercive exclusion of other providers of defense service from its territory, and all of the other depredations and coercions that are built upon these twin foci of invasions of individual rights. (Rothbard 1978, 191–92)

On this view, competing (private) providers of conflict resolution and security would serve many of the same functions that government agencies currently do.

The contrast between Nozick's position and Rothbard's is plain: both assign top priority to individual liberty, both recognize that political authority poses a potential threat to individual liberty, yet Nozick argues that *nevertheless*, some minimal level of state activity is justified, whereas Rothbard argues that *therefore*, no state is justified. Understanding, and possibly resolving, this dispute is the heart of the present inquiry.

If I am successful in arguing that minimal-state libertarianism cannot be consistent, this would by itself not yet be a full-blown defense of anarchism. Such an argument will necessarily involve the defense of the classical liberal position against more extensive liberal theories of the state, as well as the defense of the liberal tradition in general from a variety of anti-liberal theories about what sorts of considerations are important. So the full scope of what I am suggesting will depend on being persuasive in motivating both premises. In other words, since being a libertarian means that the state is only justified to the extent that it is necessary to protect people from being harmed by others, if it were shown that the state were not necessary, then it would not be justified. This, combined with a defense of libertarianism's prioritizing of individual liberty, would undermine the conceptual justification for coercive authority.

2

Coercion, State, Defense of Liberty

Before we isolate and examine the point of contention that separates libertarian minimal-statists and libertarian anarchists, we must first understand the common ground that makes the separation interesting. It will be helpful to our analysis of how they differ with regard to justifying the coercion of the state to see the shared understanding of the concepts of 'coercion' and 'state'. Indeed, it is not only instructive but crucial to observe that between the libertarian minimal-statist and the libertarian anarchist, the concepts of 'coercion' and 'state' are not in dispute, for this shared conception is in fact what makes the larger disagreement puzzling. That is, given general agreement about the nature of the state as an essentially coercive institution, and general agreement about the difficulties posed by state coercion for human freedom and autonomy, the justification of state authority by some libertarians and not others becomes problematic. In this chapter, I will explicate the concepts of 'state' and 'coercion' in order to show how all parties concerned understand them, specifically, that the state *is* regarded as essentially coercive by both libertarian minimal-statists and anarchists, and that coercion *is* seen as unacceptable to both libertarian minimal-statists and anarchists because of the conflict between coercion and the priority of freedom in libertarian theory. In the course of giving the definitions and showing that they are common to all the parties within classical liberalism, I shall also show why these theorists find state coercion objectionable, which in turn will be part of defending classical liberalism's claims about the primacy of individual liberty.

Coercion

How are we to understand coercion here? Libertarians do not all share the same conceptual analysis of coercion. One approach is to define coercion as suggested by Friedrich Hayek in *The Constitution of Liberty* (1960): coercion occurs "when one man's actions are made to serve another man's will, not for his own but for the other's purpose. . . . Coercion implies both the threat of inflicting harm and the intention thereby to bring about certain conduct" (Hayek 1960, 133). In this case, coercion would always be inconsistent with freedom. Another approach is to define coercion more simply, for example by using only the second part of Hayek's definition. Then, coercion would be justifiable in some cases (for example, to protect my rights), but not in others. This shifts the location of the moral argument, although the substance remains.

Hayek's definition of coercion is not without its critics, even among those generally sympathetic to Hayek's general project and values. Ronald Hamowy, for example, has argued that by defining 'coercion' without reference to a theory of rights, Hayek is (inadvertently) saddled with a subjective theory on which virtually anything might be said to qualify—or not.[3] In a very different approach, J.C. Lester has proposed that, rather than using 'coercion' as the contrast for 'liberty', we understand liberty as 'absence of imposed cost'. Lester's discussion of this is illuminating,[4] but it's not my intention here to resolve all disputes about the term 'coercion', nor does my argument hang on which is the best conceptual contrast for liberty. In what follows, I will be using Hayek's definition, since I think it captures what is fundamentally objectionable, that the use of force is directed towards making the other person serve the first person, but remaining mindful of the possi-

---

3. Hamowy 1978, 288.
4. As is the book in which it appears, Lester 2000.

ble conceptual disagreement.

If we, at least provisionally, accept the above account of coercion, the contrary of coerced action, then, will be voluntary action. The operative contrast will therefore be between a coerced exchange and a voluntary exchange. Choice plays a role, but not the only role, in human action. Acting to serve one's own ends is part of what distinguishes an action as freely chosen. If a robber puts a gun to one's head and demands one's money or one's life, the victim is of course choosing, in a very real sense, between two alternatives. Nevertheless, it would be a mistake to consider this a voluntary exchange. Neither alternative is designed to serve the victim's ends, but rather the robber's. Suppose Jones, preferring to be impoverished than dead, hands over his wallet. Jones has chosen to give the robber his wallet, but he has clearly not freely chosen to do so. If the same person (without any weapon) approaches Smith, and simply requests some money, Smith may choose to give him some money, or he may not. The alternative to giving this person money is, in this case, not to give money. The alternative for Jones, however, is death. This would not properly be described as 'freely choosing' to give the robber the money since the set of alternatives, giving the money or getting shot, was imposed by the robber, and neither option was an end of Jones.

H.L.A. Hart elaborates on this distinction in *The Concept of Law*. Hart describes a situation in which a gunman A has ordered B to hand over his money or be shot. This is a coercive order, so we may regard B as obliged to obey, but Hart denies that B has an obligation to obey.

> There is a difference . . . between the assertion that someone *was obliged* to do something and the assertion that he *had an obligation* to do it. The first is often a statement about the beliefs and motives with which an action is done: B was obliged to hand over his money may simply mean, as it does in the gunman case, that he believed that some harm or other unpleasant consequences would befall him if he did not hand it over and he handed it over to avoid those consequences. . . . [But this is] *not sufficient* to warrant the statement that he had an obligation to do this; it is also the case that facts of this sort,

i.e. facts about beliefs and motives are *not necessary* for the truth of a
statement that a person had an obligation to do something. (Hart
1961, 80–81, emphasis in the original)

Clearly, then, the fact that one is coerced cannot be the source of
a claim that the person has an obligation. We can imagine situations in which a person has an obligation, and then is coerced into
fulfilling that obligation, for instance a shotgun wedding, but we
will not be able to read backwards from the fact of the coercion to
the existence of an obligation. Simply avoiding the gunman A's
alternative, death, cannot provide us with reason to claim that B
was under an obligation to A. On Hart's account, being obliged
simply goes along with being coerced. Establishing obligation is a
more complicated matter.

One way to understand freedom is to think of it in terms of the
freedom to act on one's own decisions. If I am unconstrained by
others, then I am free. But this needs qualification: even if I am
unconstrained by other people, I am always 'constrained' by the
laws of nature. For instance, my 'decision' to fly like a bird is one
I cannot act on, so it's correct to say that I am not free to fly like
a bird, even though it would be odd to conclude that I am
thereby oppressed or coerced. So we might modify our conception so that we say we are free when we are constrained *only* by
natural laws, or that only the constraints *of others* can rob us of our
freedom. One is obliged to stay on the ground (on one's own
power, anyway), we might say, but not coerced. Coercion, at least
in a political context, requires a coercer who imposes a set of alternatives that will result in what the coercer wants, and clearly there
is no coercer trying to achieve some end who is responsible for
determining biological necessity. The coercer's role, defining the
situation of another, is what amounts to the denial of the
coerced's autonomy. This is something that both minimal-state
theorists and anarchists would agree is to be avoided, and at any
rate needs justification. So the coercer's role in defining the situation of the other is why we do not describe coerced actions as
voluntary. In Hart's gunman case, although the victim chose to
give up the money as opposed to suffering the consequences, this

is not a voluntary transaction because the victim's set of alternatives was determined by the gunman and neither alternative, as it turns out, was an end of the victim.

Having established that coercion requires a coercer, one might wonder if an abstraction such as 'the state' can be said to have sufficient agency to qualify as a coercer, since we have seen that, for liberals, the state is not a separately existing entity. Robert Paul Wolff addresses this concern:

> [A] sort of conceptual conjuring trick has been performed. It is clear enough who is to be the object of the force and coercion: it is the citizen, the individual whose behavior is to be altered. But the other party to the coercive interaction has somehow vanished into thin air. Rather like the Cheshire Cat, nothing is left but the state, smiling benevolently and impersonally (or perhaps malevolently, but still always impersonally). The real fact, of course, is that when a citizen is coerced, some other real flesh and blood person does the coercing, in the active voice. Not "force will be applied" but "Jones, who is a policeman or a judge or a prison guard, will apply force to Smith, who is a citizen." The state is either a real group of persons [with the requisite power] or it is a fiction. (Wolff 1976, 99)

So entities such as the state can coerce, because the actions are carried out by the human agents that comprise it.

Both minimal-state and anarchist libertarians assume a *prima facie* case against coercion; that is, they expect anyone wishing to employ coercion to justify it rather than presume that coercion is an acceptable means towards the coercer's ends. It seems plain that any given individual will consider the burden of justification to be on the coercer, namely, to explain why the individual might be interested in accepting the coercion. Is this correct?

Hayek gives one account of why we might consider coercion bad:

> He [the coerced] is not altogether deprived of the use of his capacities; but he is deprived of the possibility of using his knowledge for his own aims. . . . Most human aims can be achieved only by a chain of connected actions, decided upon as a coherent whole. . . . It is because,

and insofar as, we can predict events, or at least know probabilities, that we can achieve anything. . . . [I]f the facts which determine our plans are under the sole control of another, our actions will be similarly controlled. . . . Though the coerced will still do the best he can for himself at any given moment, the only comprehensive design that his actions fit into is that of another mind. (Hayek 1960, 134)

This objection then is two-fold: a moral element, rejecting the *fact* of the control one exercises over the other, and a practical element, concerned with the negative *effects* of the control. It is worth noting that this two-fold objection can be made either from the standpoint of the coerced individual or from the standpoint of any outside observer analyzing the situation. But from the point of view of the coerced individual there is another objection that might arise: the lack of a motivating reason to accept the coercion when the coercion conflicts with the individual's intentions. Why, one might wonder, should I allow myself to be subject to a set of alternatives imposed by another (as in your money or your life)?

A libertarian anarchist and a libertarian minimal-statist will agree about the basic argument here: human freedom is of the highest priority with regard to political values, and coercion is detrimental to human freedom, therefore coercion is something to be avoided where possible. The last part, "where possible," is what will make the two camps part company.

Hayek is quick to point out, and I think he is correct in this, that coercion does not occur in the following sort of situation: if one wants to continue to be invited to dinner at a friend's, one must "observe conventional manners" (Hayek 1960, 136). This may seem frivolous, but in fact has larger ramifications. In general, any time one wishes to obtain a benefit from another, whether it be an economic good or the pleasure of his company, one must meet certain conditions if the receipt is not to be considered theft. This is the character of voluntary exchange. In the case of obtaining toothpaste from the grocer, one must exchange money. The grocer is not forcing you to give him money, he is trading toothpaste for money. In Hayek's case of observing conventional manners of dress and speech, you are not forced by the host to behave,

you are behaving in a certain manner to get the desired benefit—
social relations. (Notice that this is a two-way street. Eccentricities
and bad tempers are forgiven in direct proportion to the degree
that person's presence is desired by the host.)

While not ordinarily characterized as a natural law theorist,
Hayek actually does address coercion and authority in a natural
law-friendly way in his distinction between imposed order and
spontaneous order. Since the spontaneous order arises out of the
many iterations of people seeking to more effectively co-ordinate
their actions and resolve disputes peaceably, then over a long
period, greater success is achieved. Coercion, especially in the form
of commands from the sovereign, is not only likely to be wrong,
but less susceptible to change on the basis of new information.
This is the thread connecting natural law theory to Hayekian spon-
taneous-order analysis.

If coercion involves the abrogation or limitation of freedom, we
will want to be clear about how Hayek is using the word 'freedom'
as well.

> It so happens that the meaning of freedom that we have adopted
> seems to be the original meaning of the word. . . . It meant always the
> possibility of a person's acting according to his own decisions and
> plans, in contrast to the position of one who was irrevocably subject
> to the will of another, who by arbitrary decision coerce him to act or
> not to act in specific ways. The time-honored phrase by which this
> freedom has often been described is therefore "independence of the
> arbitrary will of another." . . . In this sense "freedom" refers solely to
> a relation of [human beings] to other [human beings], and the only
> infringement on it is coercion by [human beings]. (Hayek 1960, 12)

Other libertarian theorists share this conception of freedom and its
value. Tibor Machan, for example, argues that

> Each man must be free to choose to gain the knowledge and perform
> the actions required for his life, i.e., if his life is to have the opportu-
> nity to be a good one, if he is to have the option between moral and
> immoral conduct, an option open to him by nature. The choice to
> learn, to judge, to evaluate, to appraise, to decide what he ought to

do in order to live his life must be each person's own, otherwise he simply has no opportunity to excel or fail at the task. His moral aspirations cannot be fulfilled (or left unfulfilled) if he is not the source of his own actions, if they are imposed or forced upon him by others. . . . The meaning of the concept "free" in the principle at issue is (must be) restricted to the absence of the restraint interference, obstruction, intervention, and so on that human beings can perpetrate. . . . Taken in the context of the present discussion, the freedom at issue is freedom to choose and act without having these obstructed by other people; the intervention at issue, in turn, is mainly physical or quasi-physical. (Machan 1975, 119)

On this account, the very condition of human life is freedom to make choices, and so coercion is seen as tantamount to the denial of the conditions necessary for human life. Hence coercion is bad in the sense of being not conducive to one's ability to live and flourish.

Douglas B. Rasmussen makes a similar argument about the relation between freedom and human life.

Coercion cannot make someone think, [or] understand, and it separates a person from his action. A person's actions cannot be his own if he has not chosen them. Coercion separates a person from his judgements and makes him act in a manner inconsistent with his own judgement. . . . Man is a material thing, not just a mind, and his fulfillment cannot be achieved if he has not the right to translate his judgements into material form. (Rasmussen 1982, 48)

Rasmussen's concern here is to ground 'natural rights' in a teleological account of human development. Rasmussen has more recently, with Douglas Den Uyl, expanded this argument in *Liberty and Nature* (1991) and *Norms of Liberty* (2005). Like Machan, Rasmussen and Den Uyl conceive of the human good in terms of growth and self-development, which is, according to his argument, impossible without political freedom. Whether rights are more coherently understood as teleological necessary conditions for human life (Machan, Rasmussen and Den Uyl), deontological side-constraints on how others may behave towards us (Nozick), or instrumental social constructs that maximize overall utility (Mill, Hayek, perhaps Narveson), is another interesting and important question which we actually need not settle in order to proceed. Ultimately, the relevant point is that whichever conception of rights one adopts, state coercion will be detrimental to securing them, and all of the theorists I am concerned with agree about that. But it is worth pausing to examine what I take to be the best defense of a theory of individual liberty, which is conceptually linked to the arguments about coercion.

What Rasmussen describes as a "neo-Aristotelian conception of human flourishing"[5] is a way of grounding classical rights theory in a theory of human nature and of moral self-development. A summary cannot do justice to the well-worked-out and elegant theory he and Den Uyl have proposed, but the idea is that for humans to develop as the sorts of beings they are, they must be free to act on their choices. We are capable of self-directed activity, and it is through the exercise of reasoned choice-making that we undertake such activity. Without the freedom to deliberate and to act on those deliberations, we would not be living fully human lives, and certainly not capable of reaching the full potential of our lives. It's also the case, the argument continues, that human lives are different, so that the best life for Smith may be in many respects different from the best life for Jones. But, first, the ability to exercise self-directed choice is a shared requirement for both Smith and Jones, despite the differences, and second, these differences will only flourish under a social structure founded on a principle of liberty. Hence,

> rights are based on the recognition that being self-directed or autonomous is something which is right in itself and that protecting the possibility of self-directedness or autonomy is the objective requirement to be met for producing a compossible set of moral territories consistent with the individualized and self-directed character of human flourishing.[6]

---

5. Rasmussen 1999.
6. Rasmussen and Den Uyl 1991, 115.

In other words, on the neo-Aristotelian ethic, the human good is individualized yet objective, and a rights-based social structure is the necessary condition of securing both aspects of that. 'Human nature' as a generic rubric provides generic parameters for flourishing, but the plural and agent-relative nature of human flourishing make it the sort of thing that can only be realized in a context of freedom to act, not in a coercive environment. There's more to moral philosophy than rights, but a social order of rights is the necessary precondition of moral action, of human self-development. It is what allows for the possibilities of different flourishings without creating moral conflict ('compossibility').

Rasmussen and Den Uyl thus conceive of rights as being "meta-normative" principles, as opposed to normative, in that they do not specify ends as such, but merely the conditions under which pursuit of ends is legitimate. This is, for them, a foundation from which to derive a regime of liberty. Recognition of others as rights-bearing produces a social order in which all are free to pursue their ends, to the extent that they are not violating the rights of others. Rasmussen and Den Uyl argue that human flourishing depends on the development of virtue, and this requires a political culture of freedom. Their strategy avoids both radical moral subjectivism and the tendency towards political totalitarianism. It is a 'natural rights' approach, but not in the Lockean sense of the rights being some thing in nature. The rights are natural in the sense of 'derived from a conception of human nature'.

On this view, rights should not be conceived of as exhaustive guides to moral conduct, but as the precondition for moral activity—the precondition of self-directed development of the person. Rights protect the possibility of self-directedness in a social setting. If the human good is plural and agent-relative, rights protect diversity. The social dimension of human flourishing is not an argument against individual rights—it's why we need individual rights. This creates a space for each to develop and pursue projects subject to the constraint of allowing the same space for others. A social order of rights respects both individuality and sociality.

If the application of practical reason to self-directed action is a necessary condition of human flourishing, then people need to be free to develop and pursue their ends. This pursuit will be bounded by the compossibility criterion, that such pursuits do not infringe on others' attempts to do the same. A social order of individual rights is what translates this into practice. Maximizing the opportunities for self-directed action means minimizing the opportunities for coercion, hence liberty as a necessary condition for human flourishing.

In their most recent formulation of the argument, *Norms of Liberty*, Rasmussen and Den Uyl wisely avoid the word 'state', preferring the more cumbersome but less loaded 'political/legal order'. But that's just the question: does this model of liberty justify a state? Does it necessitate a state? Or can the liberty here defended be secured in some kind of 'political/legal order' which isn't a state? Rasmussen and Den Uyl phrase the question this way: "How are we to avoid the anarchist's condemnation of political/legal life as necessarily requiring the sacrifice of some form of the good life to other forms?" (p. 84). Actually, though, it is not political/legal life *per se* which does this, it is only the statist version of that life. The distinction between 'state' and 'some kind of political/legal order' is not at all trivial, and it is certainly not mere semantics. Rasmussen's and Den Uyl's choice to avoid the word 'state', while prudent, leaves open a key question which needs to be answered at some point, namely, whether the state (even the minimal state) is legitimate.

Libertarian theorists do not all base their defense of the priority of liberty on the same ethical foundations, but for any conception of the importance of freedom there will be a related understanding of how coercion is detrimental to freedom. Jan Narveson puts it this way:

> [N]ot to be at liberty is to be unable to do what we want to do, to achieve our ends, to realize our values—in short, to live, in this respect or that, our lives. (Narveson 1988, 15)

This view leads him to conclude that "freedom is fundamentally the freedom to *determine*, namely, to determine what is the case. . . . 'Person A is [completely] free with respect to S' = 'S obtains if and only if A chooses that S'" (Narveson 1988, 18; brackets and emphasis in original). On this account, coercion

> is a matter of bringing it about that the coerced person's alternatives are considerably worse than in the status quo ante, and that some of the ways of making them worse will be interferences with his or her freedom if they are performed. (Narveson 1988, 35)

So coercion is a *prima facie* wrong for both minimal-state and anarchist libertarians, although there is some variation in emphasis in the way it is described. Coercion can then be seen by all of these theorists as something requiring justification. Such justification will only emerge in Narveson's argument with regard to "wrongful freedom, which *can* be legitimately interfered with" (Narveson 1988, 35), which refers to the restriction on the use of coercive force to stopping people from interfering with each others' freedom (Narveson 1988, 50).

We can recognize a morally significant distinction between using force in self-defense and initiating force against another, which is the distinction Narveson is appealing to here. On this view, what is objectionable is the initiation of force against another, which provides justification for defensive force. To justify coercion, then, one would need to show that it was responsive, not initial. Minimal-statist libertarians will argue that there are conditions which require, and therefore legitimate, the use of coercion by the political authority. This will be at the heart of the dispute.

The concept of coercion implies a coercer who forces the coerced to make a decision to suit the ends of the coercer and not the ends of the coerced. Of course, when given a choice between one's money and one's life, choosing not to die may serve one's ends, but the decision is being imposed by the brigand for his own ends, where no decision would otherwise be made. A voluntary transaction necessarily involves an exchange of goods or services that serves the perceived ends of both parties. So while a coerced transaction might or might not benefit the coerced, it undoubtedly benefits the coercer, for the coercer must perceive some gain as the result of his application of coercion.

Can paternalistic coercion be seen in this light, or is it a counter-example? Paternalistic coercion is said to occur when the purported justification of the coercion is that it is for the coerced's 'own good'. Thus the coerced is being forced to act or forbear against his will, but the benefit to the coercer is not clear. Nevertheless, the coercer must have some interest in the outcome of the coercion in order to have bothered with it in the first place. We can see this by examining both an example of private paternalistic coercion and an example of state paternalistic coercion. For the former, consider a parent forcing a child to eat a healthy meal. Clearly the parent benefits from this coercion to the extent that it produces a healthier child. This is a benefit if we assume that the parent values having healthy children. When the state engages in paternalistic coercion, it is less obvious how it benefits the state, but consider any paternalistic law. The justification is always phrased in terms of a 'compelling state interest'. Indeed, for legal paternalism to be a legitimate principle of a regime requires that the regime claim to have an interest in the well-being of the subjects in precisely the same manner as the parent has in the child's.

So at the simplest level, paternalistic state coercion can be said to benefit the state by its very nature of assuming the familial role. At a more complex level of analysis, the actual rulers responsible for the paternalist legislation are benefiting to the extent that they increase the scope of their own power over the subjects, regardless of the fact that the subjects may also benefit from the paternalist legislation. Therefore paternalist coercion may also be seen as producing a benefit to the coercer. The key notion, however, remains the idea that the actions of the coerced are made to serve another's ends, even though these may occasionally coincide with the coerced's ends, regardless of any benefits that might be obtained by either party. As a concrete example, consider laws requiring motorcyclists to wear helmets. This may benefit a motorcyclist if it protects him from more serious head injury, but it also benefits the state, since (in our society) there is a cost to taxpayers involved in a person's head injury.

More importantly (for our purposes), minimal-state theorists and anarchist theorists share a rejection of coercion as a legitimate political activity. Robert Nozick tells us at the beginning of his 1974 book *Anarchy, State, and Utopia* that "Since I begin with a strong formulation of individual rights, I treat seriously the anarchist claim that ... the state must violate individuals' rights and hence is intrinsically immoral" (Nozick 1974, xi). Nozick's criticism of taxation as being "on a par with forced labor" (Nozick 1974, 169) is only a criticism if he believes forced labor to be an objectionable thing. We would notice the same underlying assumption if we were to consider why the following is meant to be a criticism of patterned schemes of distributive justice: "[N]o end-state principle or distributional patterned principle of justice can be continuously realized without continuous interference with people's lives" (Nozick 1974, 163). Nozick demonstrates this with the "Wilt Chamberlain" example: say we begin with any patterned distribution of resources one chooses—Rawlsian, egalitarian, whatever—then imagine that there is one basketball player who is sufficiently interesting that many people are happy to pay an extra twenty-five cents to see him play (Nozick 1974, p. 160). In short order, Wilt Chamberlain will be vastly wealthy and the pattern will be upset. The only way to preserve the pattern will be to forcibly prohibit the many private, voluntary transactions that have led to this new state of affairs. Since the new inequality is entirely the result of people's choices to dispose of their resources as they see fit, it isn't clear how it could be unjust, but if it is, then liberty must be a dispensable concept.

Tibor Machan puts it this way in his *Individuals and Their Rights*: "*chosen* conduct of the agent that attains his or her happiness, is a vital element of the human happiness that a good human community ought to facilitate for all" (Machan 1989, xiv, emphasis in the original). Jan Narveson says that the "central libertarian complaint" is that "you have no choice but to deal with . . . the Government; and this is not in the sense that your particular Government is the only one that happened to be around, but rather that it was the only one *allowed* to be around" (Narveson 1988, 211). In each case, the denial of autonomy, the abrogation of individual freedom, and the reduction or removal of choice through the use of force or its threat, is presumed by the writers to be something to be avoided, or at the very least which needs to be justified in some way. The concept of coercion, then, is not the main point of contention between libertarian minimal-statists and libertarian anarchists. That freedom is good for people to have is a common value.

The State

Before we can discuss the legitimacy of the state, we should be clear in our conception of what the state is. The anarchist is going to claim that society is a good thing even though the state is a bad thing.[7] Therefore the distinction between society—the state of affairs consisting in people living together, and the state—a political entity with a particular role and various powers, will be a crucial one. As we shall see, it is only certain features of the state that are objected to by anarchists, particularly the state's reliance on coercion. One question to ask, then, is whether or not coercion may be seen as an intrinsic feature of the state, and indeed, examining the concept of the state will make the anarchist objection to it quite clear.

Murray Rothbard, a libertarian anarchist, defines the state as having two distinct, defining, features.

> (1) [I]t acquires its income by the physical coercion known as "taxation"; and (2) it asserts and usually obtains a coerced monopoly of the provision of defense service (police and courts) over a given territorial area. (Rothbard 1978, 191)

Though some find the blunt and emphatic language off-putting, this turns out to be a useful definition. Robert Nozick appeals to a similar account of the state when he explains why an individualist

---

7. Hence the title of Rothbard's 1978 article, "Society Without a State." The point is that the anarchists we are concerned with think that there is something beneficial, perhaps even necessary, about living in some species of community, both for social and economic reasons. Hence criticisms are of coercive, monopolistic practices intrinsic to government, not the brute fact of living with other people.

anarchist such as Rothbard might have a *prima facie* case against the state.

> For [the individualist anarchist] holds that when the state monopolizes the use of force in a territory and punishes others who violate its monopoly, and when the state provides protection for everyone by forcing some to purchase protection for others, it violates side constraints on how individuals may be treated. (Nozick 1974, 51)

Jan Narveson conceives of the state in a similar way. The state "(1) has a monopoly of force . . . and (2) it caters to everyone within its area, whether they like it or not, distributing the costs of doing so among its other clients in cases of inability to pay" (Narveson 1988, 219). All these writers, on the other hand, mean by 'society' simply the state of affairs consisting in people's living amongst each other, trading goods and labor, having personal relations, engaging in mutually advantageous endeavors, and so on.

Taxation figures prominently, indeed as a defining feature, in most libertarian accounts of the state not only because it is itself coercive, but also because it serves as the means to accomplish the state's other ends, whatever those happen to be. Why does taxation loom so large in these theories?

> The crucial role of taxation may be seen in the fact that the state is the only institution or organization which regularly and systematically acquires its income through the use of physical coercion. All other individuals or organizations acquire their income voluntarily. (Rothbard 1978, 192)

Naturally, libertarians object to other coercive features of the state as well, for example military conscription or government suppression of newspapers. The point is that taxation makes all other government activities possible, and is itself, according to the argument, coercive.

First of all, does taxation involve coercion? Given our earlier account of coercion, it seems clear that it does, as long as the taxation is not voluntary. If the taxation in question were strictly voluntary, then of course it would be false to claim that it involved coercion. However, we do not generally speak of voluntarily submitted fees for goods or services as taxes. If the money is involuntarily submitted, it must have involved coercion (keeping in mind that coercion can consist in the threat of force as well as the actual use of force). Of course it is true that the taxpayer benefits to some extent from the taxation, but this does not alter the coercive nature of the transaction. We earlier defined coercion as being forced to serve another's ends, so the involuntariness of the arrangement is what marks it as coercive.

Nozick describes taxation not strictly as theft, but more akin to forced labor. "Taking the earnings of *n* hours labor is like taking *n* hours from the person; it is like forcing the person to work *n* hours for another's purpose" (Nozick 1974, 169). He points out that if any theory asserting that a man may be forced to labor for *n* hours to serve others would be illiberal, then appropriating the fruits of *n* hours labor must also be illiberal (Nozick 1974, 170). Although one might argue that one works the *n* hours to serve oneself through the agency of others, such as police officers, judges, and so forth, this is clearly only a partial description of what is involved. What needs to be added is the fact that one has not necessarily chosen to do this.

More broadly, Nozick's point is that the Rawlsian distinction between political liberty and economic liberty is fallacious. The upshot of his famous "Wilt Chamberlain" example is that the exercise of economic liberty is a manifestation of the political freedom to act on our individuality. To restrict the exercise of economic liberty is to restrict one's ability to act autonomously to serve one's own ends. If my labor may be compelled, then I do not enjoy full self-ownership.

Another way of understanding the coercive element intrinsic to taxation may be found by examining the criminal law. It is no surprise that the issue of taking someone's property by coercion is treated by the criminal law, since most people in fact believe it to be wrong to coerce another to get something from him. (I quote here from the Penal Code of New York; most other jurisdictions have similar codes.) The account given here of larceny by extortion is explicit with regard to the sense of coercion implied, and it is exactly the same as the one I have been using.

1: A person steals property and commits larceny when, with intent to deprive another of property or appropriate the same to himself or a third person, he wrongfully takes, obtains, or withholds such property from an owner thereof. 2. Larceny includes a wrongful taking, obtaining, or withholding of another's property with the intent proscribed in section 1 of this section, committed in any of the following ways: . . . e. By extortion. A person obtains property by extortion when he compels or induces another person to deliver such property to himself or a third person by means of instilling in him a fear that if the property is not so delivered, the actor or another will: . . . i. Cause physical injury to some person in the future, . . . iv. Accuse some person of a crime or cause criminal charges to be instituted against him, . . . viii. Use or abuse his position as a public servant by performing some act within or related to his official duties or by failing or refusing to perform one of his official duties in such a manner as to affect some person adversely, . . . ix. Perform any other act which would not in itself benefit the actor but which is calculated to harm another person materially with respect to his health, safety, business, calling, career, financial condition, reputation, or personal relationship. (New York Penal Code, Section 155.05)

With one exception, this is precisely what taxation involves. The one exception is the word "wrongfully" above, since the state's activity is presumptively rightful. The coerced transfer, then, is larceny by extortion if it is wrongful, and not larceny, presumably, if it is rightful. If the difference between rightful and wrongful is not to be a matter of begging the question, it will have to involve, at least from the point of view of someone such as Nozick, serving the perceived ends of the parties to the exchange. Obviously, a voluntary exchange would be considered rightful by any minimal-state libertarian, since both parties are serving their own ends, but are there any conditions under which an involuntary exchange would be considered rightful?

The fact that others intentionally intervene, in violation of a side constraint against aggression, to threaten force to limit the alternatives . . . to paying taxes or [being punished], makes the taxation system one of forced labor. (Nozick 1974, 169)

For theorists such as Nozick and Machan, consent and voluntariness are crucial components of the rightness of a transaction. Since taxation fails these tests, one would expect them to oppose the practice conceptually, even if they accept it for other reasons, perhaps that it is necessary to accomplish some other end. This is in fact the case.

If we cannot make a case for an implicit consent to the transfer of the money, then we will have to regard taxation as an illegitimate transaction, one made under coercion. I shall address below the conception of a 'tacit' consent to the taxation, but a common assumption, even among minimal-state libertarians, who object conceptually to taxation, is that taxation is necessary for the existence of their minimal state. However, this begs the question, for what we are concerned with here is the putative necessity of the state. But in any event it seems clear that the first element of Rothbard's definition of the state is present in minimal-state libertarian accounts. We shall return in the next chapter to why minimal-state theorists find themselves accepting a practice that they disapprove of in principle.

The second element of Rothbard's definition of the state is the state's assertion of a coerced monopoly of the provision of defense and arbitration services over geographical territories. Nozick also finds this a necessary condition of something's being a state.[8] "A state . . . says that only it may decide who may use force and under what conditions; it reserves to itself the sole right to pass on the legitimacy and permissibility of any use of force within its boundaries; furthermore it claims the right to punish all those who violate its claimed monopoly" (Nozick 1974, 23). Is this true?

It seems uncontroversial to suggest that the state has a monopoly on these services. However, there are various private security companies, such as Brink's, or the security force of any large university. Does the existence of such companies mean that the state

---

8. On the other hand, Nozick says, formulating *sufficient* conditions for the existence of the state "turns out to be a difficult and messy task" (Nozick 1974, 23).

does not enjoy a 'coercive monopoly of power'? Since all of these companies are subordinate to the authority of the state, the answer is no. The state's authority and the state's monopoly are not diminished by the various firms. The (private) university security guard, for instance, is only empowered to act as a surrogate for the agent of the state. By this I mean that a security guard cannot imprison a thief, (although he can arrest someone just like any other citizen). The university that employs him cannot establish laws that conflict with the state's. For example, the university may 'legislate' that no men may be in the women's dorm after 9:30, and if any are found the security guard would be empowered to remove them. This works because the dorm in question is private property, so the guard is acting in accordance with the overall law of the land. By contrast, this private university may not legalize marijuana. The building owner's policies may not themselves be in violation of city, state, or federal law.

Similarly, the existence of a variety of law-enforcement agencies such as city police, state police, and the F.B.I does not qualify as a counter-example to the claim that the state has a monopoly on the provision of defense and arbitration services over a geographical monopoly, for two reasons. The first reason is the same as in the case of the university security guard: the city can make no laws that override state laws, and states can make no laws which conflict with federal laws. For example, since kidnapping is a federal offense, the Rhode Island legislature cannot legalize it. Since the Commonwealth of Pennsylvania has set the drinking age at twenty-one, Philadelphia cannot set it at twenty. (And because Philadelphia police are obliged to enforce state laws as well as local laws, Jack's Bar cannot set its own drinking age at twenty.) In other words, elaborations are permitted, but the lesser jurisdiction cannot contradict the higher.

The second reason is that the F.B.I, city police, and state police actually have the same 'employer'—the government. We speak of 'levels of government' or 'branches of the government' precisely because they are all parts of a whole. The United States Constitution, for example, is the 'supreme law of the land'. The non-conflicting-laws condition of the previous two examples exists because of this unity of government. In other words, the unity of the government is *why* Pennsylvania law cannot contradict Federal law. Government can be divided up in various ways, but its power is nevertheless univocal. The ideas of federalism and separation of powers have their roots in an attempt to reduce the scope of government power over the individual. So from a long view, the fact that we have separate branches and levels of government *is* liberty-enhancing, relative to systems like monarchy or communism. But the government as a whole is nevertheless, as Narveson puts it, the only one allowed to exist.

That is not to say that the government is all-encompassing. Many contractual disputes, for example, are addressed in private arbitration, if both parties had a prior agreement to this. But the government's use of force is unique, and private arbitration contracts cannot include penalties which violate the law of the land, just as they cannot mandate or permit conduct which violates the law of the land (as in the case of prostitution).

Must all states have these characteristics of monopoly control and the use of coercion, or is it possible to have a state that does not? One answer is that states have these features by definition, so any thing which lacked them would fail automatically to be a state. The more interesting answer is that something which was said to be a state, but was in fact *not* a coercively maintained monopoly of power, would not be the sort of state (or not enough of a state) to generate the objections of the anarchist. In other words, any social association that did not have those features would not be the sort of thing that an anarchist would object to, and if it is to be called a state anyway, then the word 'anarchist' would need a new definition. In any event, existing states *do* have these two features, so a semantic dispute at this stage would not be productive, although we might pause for a moment to consider the conception of a 'morally legitimate' state in the theories of some minimal-state libertarians, which will be relevant in considering how an anarchist might respond to those arguments. In Machan's view, for instance,

> the justification and need of government arises from the objective value to all members of society of living with others without . . . the

general insecurity that goes with lawlessness. Individuals who recognize the value of social life readily acknowledge the value of establishing an agency to provide them with the protection and preservation of their rights in the context of a system of objective law. (Machan 1982, 204)

Government activities could therefore, theoretically, be provided on a fee-for-service basis. Since the government, on this view, is only in the business of adjudicating conflicts, protecting rights, and securing contracts, and since one could choose not to employ the government's services for most of these, funding for these activities could occur non-coercively, by having users of a service bear its costs. This state would still, according to Machan, have to stop others, such as an alternative provider of rights protection, from offering the services the government offers. Machan argues that this cannot be helped, and we will examine his arguments for this in the next chapter. But assuming his arguments about the 'natural' monopoly of government on conflict resolution are valid, then the state he describes would be as non-coercive as possible. This is not a successful dismissal of the anarchist position. The anarchist argument is that although society is a good thing, coercion is a bad thing, and states as we know them essentially involve coercion. A state that employed no coercion, or as little as possible for society to exist, would not be the same state that anti-statists are against. Indeed, the whole point of contention turns out to be over this last qualifier, that since just a little coercion is required for society to exist, therefore the minimal state is justified, which is the dispute at the heart of Chapter 3.

The important point, however, is that minimal-state libertarians regard state power as a thing that needs to be justified *because* of its coercive features. This is a conception shared with anarchists. We have seen that both minimal-state libertarians and anarchist libertarians view the state as a political entity which essentially involves coercion, coercion is seen as detrimental to human freedom, and freedom is to receive the highest priority among political values when developing a theory. The anarchist criticism, then, is that *given* this view of coercion and state power, such a justification cannot be provided coherently. No state could possibly be legitimate on this view. Why do some libertarians, then, attempt to provide a justification for the state, and how successful are these attempts given the shared conceptions and values that generate the anarchist's *prima facie* objection? In Chapter 3, I shall examine what I take to be the common presumption that motivates the justification of state authority for theorists who ordinarily would be predisposed against the state. This should help determine whether the anarchist criticism is well-founded. Having done that, Chapter 4 will be concerned with how libertarian anarchists respond to the concerns of libertarians who defend the state.

3

The Hobbesian Fear

More theories of political authority revolve around what I shall describe as a "Hobbesian Fear" than is realized even by the theorists who create them. By this I mean that a Hobbesian Fear is often an implicit rather than an explicit premise in arguments justifying the authority of the state. My first task is to explain what a Hobbesian Fear is. Afterwards, I shall be able to demonstrate the role it plays in various theories of state coercion, and the importance of this role.

Simply stated, a Hobbesian Fear is the notion that political authority is necessary for society to exist; more specifically, that political authority is the only way to secure enforcement of contracts and is therefore a necessary condition of the social cooperation that is essential for life. If we did not have a government, the argument has it, we would find ourselves at each others' throats. This concern is an essential element of Thomas Hobbes's argument for the justification of the sovereign in Chapter 13 of *Leviathan*: "During the time men live without a common Power to keep them all in awe, they are in that condition which is called War . . . of every man, against every man." Hobbes stipulates that by "war," he need not mean actual fighting, but only the known disposition to fighting "during all the time there is no assurance to the contrary." The accompanying argument can be summarized along these lines:

**a. Equality of natural endowments and mental powers
leads to equality of hope in attaining our ends** (given the central place in Hobbes's political theory of the desire for self-preservation and the desire for the means of a commodious existence).
Hobbes does not mean that all are exactly equal in every way:

> Nature hath made men so equall, in the faculties of body and mind;
> as that though there be found one man sometimes manifestly stronger
> in body, or of quicker mind than another; yet when all is reckoned
> together, the difference between man, and man, is not so consider-
> able, as that one man can thereupon claim to himself any benefit, to
> which another may not pretend, as well as he. For as to the strength
> of body, the weakest has strength enough to kill the strongest, either
> by secret machination, or by confederacy with others, that are in the
> same danger with himself. (Hobbes 1651, 183)

This establishes an equality sufficient for everyone to be in fear of
everyone else.

**b. Furthermore, equality of hope, given the scarcity of nat-
ural and produced means of life, puts people in competition
with one another and makes them potential enemies.**

> And therefore if any two men desire the same thing, which neverthe-
> less they cannot both enjoy, they become enemies; and in the way to
> their End . . . endeavour to destroy, or subdue one another. (Hobbes
> 1651, 184)

**c. Competition, given the great uncertainty concerning the
aims of others and the possibility of their forming alliances
and coalitions against us, gives rise to "diffidence," in other
words to a state of general distrust.**
**d. This general distrust, made greater by the possibility
that others may be moved to gain dominion by "pride and
vainglory," together with the fact that no covenants can provide security in the absence of an enforcer of some sort, makes
productive industry seem less worthwhile and predation more
productive, and leads people to believe that their security is**

best secured by anticipatory attack (Hobbes 1651, 185).

e. Anticipation, as the state of affairs in which the disposition to strike first when the circumstances seem propitious is generally and publicly known, is, by Hobbes's definition, a State of War.

Gregory S. Kavka elaborates:

(1) Anticipation is a more reasonable strategy for individuals to follow in the state of nature than is lying low. (2) But universal war and misery is the inevitable result of the individuals in the state of nature following the anticipation strategy. (3) The parties in the state of nature joining together into defensive groups merely moves the main anticipatory violence from the interpersonal level to the intergroup level. (4) Only leaving the state of nature by forming a civil society can provide security to the parties and avoid the problems posed by the logic of escalating anticipation. (5) The problems encountered in an appropriate kind of civil society are less severe than the problems of insecurity and anticipation in the state of nature. (6) Therefore, rational parties in the state of nature would form a civil society of an appropriate kind in order to leave that state of nature. (Kavka 1986, 108–09)

From this argument, "it is manifest," according to Hobbes, that the alternative to political authority is total war. Hobbes sees the sovereign as guarantor of a sort of "social contract" that lifts mankind out of the state of perpetual war of all against all that is the state of nature into a state in which people can develop and pursue their ends and so on - a civil society.

According to Jean Hampton (1986), Hobbes thinks that cooperation is possible in the state of nature—but also highly risky.

Whether or not one should take the risk depends on the probability that one's partner will renege, the extent of the damage his reneging will inflict, and the probability, if he does renege, that he can be educated by one's cooperation to cooperate himself in the future. . . . In high-risk situations, contract keeping will be too dangerous for a person who is committed to self-preservation. And in low-risk situations, Hobbes could insist that the widespread shortsightedness of

the natural state's inhabitants will make the probability of one's partner reneging and failing to learn anything from one's own cooperative act high enough that an expected-utility calculation likely will
dictate against cooperation. (Hampton 1986, 83)

Indeed, even if some do cooperate and learn about cooperation, all
that Hobbes needs to have be the case for the state of nature to
lead to the state of total war is that reneging on contractual
arrangements is sufficiently widespread to erode social institutions,
because this will be sufficient to activate the 'pre-emptive attack'
clause of his formula.

The intuitive appeal of this argument rests on the common
sense of the claim that society would be impossible if we were all
attacking each other. One of the crucial assumptions here is the
claim that covenants cannot provide security in the absence of
some sort of enforcement mechanism, explicitly stated in Chapter
14 of *Leviathan*. It seems clear enough that recognizably civil society, one which permitted people to develop and pursue their ends
and so on, would be impossible given the total war of all against
all. What is problematic is the claim that the *state* is necessary in
order to avoid this situation. In Chapter 17, Hobbes explains the
aim and function of government:

> [Men] getting themselves out from that miserable condition of War,
> which is necessarily consequent (as hath been shewn) to the natural
> Passions of men, when there is no visible Power to keep them in awe,
> and tie them by fear of punishment to the performance of their
> covenants. (Hobbes 1651, 223)

This then is the concern that in later theorists I will refer to as a
Hobbesian Fear: that without a government, we cannot have society, for we will lack the very thing that makes it possible, namely,
a mechanism for cooperation enforcement.

If cooperation enforcement *can* be provided in the absence of
political authority, then this Hobbesian Fear is mistaken: political
authority is *not* a necessary condition of society. Any theory of justification of the state that has as its root a Hobbesian Fear would
then lack a convincing foundation. Next we shall examine the

extent to which even minimal-state libertarians rely on a Hobbesian Fear, and then we shall go on to investigate various anarchist responses to the challenge.

Since libertarian minimal-statists can arrive at libertarianism in different ways, do they all arrive at their defense of the minimal state in different ways? I think that inasmuch as they address the issue at all, they in fact have what I have described as a "Hobbesian Fear" as a common underlying principle (even if some do not explicitly acknowledge it). I shall examine positive arguments for the state from representative theorists from different identifiable approaches to minimal-state liberalism.

Libertarianism Based in Efficiency

Nozick's book *Anarchy, State, and Utopia* (1974) is well-known for its appeal to natural rights. The first sentence in the book simply and straightforwardly lets the reader know where the author stands on this issue: "Individuals have rights, and there are things no person or group may do to them (without violating their rights)" (Nozick 1974, ix). It is this conception of rights as moral "side-constraints" on activity that underlies much of his critiques of Marxism and Rawlsian liberalism. To avoid falling into the trap Machan would later criticize others for, not bothering to justify the state, Nozick devotes the first 146 pages to explaining how the minimal state "could arise" without violating anyone's rights before he proceeds to explain how any more extensive state would do just this. However, his arguments against anarchism (his arguments positively justifying the state) are *not* completely grounded in his conception of natural rights (although rights play a role).

The primary consideration in Nozick's account of the minimal state is efficiency. As I read him, the services of protection and conflict resolution would be provided more efficiently with the minimal state than without it, and thus the state is inevitable. He defends the extension of the right to individual self-defense to one of collective self-defense in the sense that many might collectively engage the same means of exercising their right to self-protection, which means it would be morally legitimate to pay other people or companies to protect us. Then Nozick explains how, as a matter of economic efficiency, one of these protective agencies would come to dominate the others, at least in a particular geographic area, through a non-coercive process of mergers and acquisitions. This "dominant protective agency" would then fit the standard definitions of a state, as it provides protection for all and monopolizes this service, but would also satisfy the "moral objections of the individualist anarchist" (Nozick 1974, 114) because it arose in a way that did not violate anyone's rights. This sounds like a rights-based argument, but it is not (that is, this component of his work is not).

The claim that the dominant protective agency "would" arise by an "invisible-hand process" is a claim, almost a prediction, about the structure of the initially-arising market in protection services. Competing services are not ruled out *a priori*; rather he thinks that stability and other market conditions will generate the dominant protective agency. This is an argument about markets, not rights. He assumes that protection is an example of a service that naturally tends towards an "efficient monopoly," meaning a monopoly which does not depend on government coercion as the barrier to competition which might threaten it. This *may* be the case, although perhaps we ought not to treat it as a given. Let us assume for the moment that this is so. Nozick says the protection of "independents" who do not want to subscribe to the dominant protective agency might be subsidized by members of the dominant protective agency who pay a higher fee for a different kind of service. In any event, though, Nozick argues that it would not be rights-violating for this "de facto monopoly" to coerce payment for the services. Presumably he arrives at this conclusion because each of the smaller protection agencies was voluntarily funded, so the new 'parent company' is not violating rights to exact payment after the 'merger'. The question, then, is whether or not coercion is involved *after* the formation of the dominant protective agency. If someone who, despite having voluntarily subscribed to one of the smaller companies, disliked the operation of the new dominant protective agency wanted to 'opt out', would this be permitted by the agency? Would he be entitled to secure this service from someone else? If the dominant protective agency must use coercion to bar market entry of competing services, and may force dissenters to continue paying them, then Nozick will be in error in claiming that no rights have been violated. (And if one *can* opt out of what is simply the largest provider of the service, then Nozick's vision will be indistinguishable from Rothbard's conception of a society without a state.)

The only remaining justification would be a concern that 'permitting' entry into this market would mean that everyone's rights would be made less secure by the competition between protective agencies, and that therefore it is not wrong to prohibit this. Nozick develops this idea by arguing that these companies would be inclined to find their interests best served by pre-emptive attack, and that the known proclivity towards striking first when this seemed advantageous would, at the least, weaken everyone's ability to protect their rights, and at worst destroy society.

> A protective agency dominant in a territory does satisfy the two crucial necessary conditions for being a state. It is the only generally effective enforcer of a prohibition on others' using unreliable enforcement procedures [that is, independent enforcement] . . . And the agency protects those nonclients in its territory whom it prohibits from using self-help enforcement . . . even if such protection must be financed (in apparent redistributive fashion) by its clients. It is morally required to do this by the principle of compensation, which requires those who act in self-protection in order to increase their own security to compensate those they prohibit from doing risky acts which might have turned out to be harmless [i.e., seeking independent enforcement] for the disadvantages imposed on them. (Nozick 1974, 113–14)

It makes sense to argue that *if* the dominant protective agency may prohibit private enforcement on the grounds that its members feel that private enforcement is risky and makes them less secure, *then* the agency must compensate those so prohibited. But why should the dominant protective agency prohibit? Because, Nozick says, private enforcement entails not chaos, but the risk of chaos. "An independent might be prohibited from privately exacting

justice because his procedure is known to be too risky and dangerous . . . or because his procedure isn't known not to be risky"
(Nozick 1974, 88). "Our rationale for this prohibition rests on the
ignorance, uncertainty, and lack of knowledge of people. . . .
Disagreements about what is to be enforced . . . provide yet
another reason (in addition to lack of factual knowledge) for the
apparatus of the state." (Nozick 1974, 140–41). It is clear that this
argument relies on, and in fact is an example of, what I have
described as a Hobbesian Fear. So the soundness of Nozick's argument for the legitimacy of the state rests on the implicit or explicit
acceptance of the Hobbesian Fear as a real concern.

Libertarianism from Natural Rights Theory

Tibor Machan's arguments for the justification of state authority
anticipate the aforementioned anarchist criticism, so they predomi-
nantly involve criticism of anarchist theories. Conversely, his rec-
ommendations concerning the limitations of government along
libertarian lines anticipates welfarist and socialist responses and
involve criticisms of those theories. This work will not be concerned
with that aspect of his theory, but it is worth noticing that this
approach is the same strategy used by Nozick (1974), but by few if
any other minimal-state libertarians. Machan finds the paucity of
liberal theories that use this strategy unfortunate, and criticizes such
theorists: "Dworkin [for example] never establishes government's
authority to govern but merely specifies some checks on its rule"
(Machan 1983, 515). The fact that so many liberals, even minimal
statists, argue in this manner is, I believe, testimony to the extent to
which a Hobbesian Fear dominates political theory.

In *Human Rights and Human Liberties*, Machan's argument
for the legitimacy of the state addresses both Robert Paul Wolff's
"Kantian anarchism" and Murray Rothbard's "individualist anarchism." His criticism of Wolff centers around the claim that the
morally legitimate state exists just to protect the personal autonomy that Wolff thinks rules out the state. Therefore, although
Wolff has a legitimate complaint against the state-as-it-often-
appears, he has none against the state that Machan is recommend-

ing—a state the sole functions of which consist of protecting rights, a morally legitimate state. Machan thus assumes that something called 'the state' is necessary for the protection of rights. This assumption is precisely what is being assailed by Rothbard. (I assume that Machan allows himself this assumption in his discussion of Wolff because he will more explicitly argue for it in his subsequent discussion of Rothbard.)

Wolff argues that

> The defining mark of the state is authority, the right to rule. The primary obligation of man is autonomy, the refusal to be ruled. It would seem, then, that there can be no resolution of the conflict between the autonomy of the individual and the putative authority of the state. . . . In that sense, it would seem that anarchism is the only political doctrine consistent with the virtue of autonomy. (Wolff 1970, 18)

Wolff's emphasis on individual autonomy, and his concern that this is abridged when political freedom is curtailed, is shared by Machan. Machan acknowledges this even as he explains that the conflict Wolff mentions *can* be resolved.

> One reason Wolff's thesis is important for us is that it expresses a position *which might be taken to follow from one put forth in these pages.* . . . In response let me explain that Wolff's argument might be valid against any form of legal authorization to prescribe conduct having no bearing on the lives of others, private conduct that does not unavoidably involve others. . . . [But] when government is viewed as a hired agent . . . it does not necessarily imply that its commands deprive a person of his moral autonomy and authority. (Machan 1975, 145, emphasis added)

Machan's argument here is that the government may be seen as an authorized agent, assisting people in the maintenance of their autonomy by protecting their rights. "Wolff's defense of anarchism does not undercut the efforts of those who aim to devise a legal system . . . in accordance with human rights. It is precisely for purposes of *protection* of individual moral autonomy that such a system would be devised" (Machan 1975, 146). Machan's approach here is reminiscent of the nineteenth-century French theorist Bastiat, who argues that the law (in a morally legitimate state) is the "collective organization of the individual right to lawful defense" (Bastiat 1850, 6). Bastiat's argument goes as follows:

> If every person has the right to defend—even by force—his person, his liberty, and his property, then it follows that a group of men have the right to organize and support a common force to protect these rights constantly. (Bastiat 1850, 6)

It may indeed follow that they have this right, but it does not follow that all persons are bound to join this organization on pain of compulsion, unless of course this is seen as a necessary condition of societal existence, which would be the case only given that what I have termed the Hobbesian Fear is warranted.

As Wolff's primary objection to the state is the threat it poses to individual autonomy, Machan identifies Rothbard's primary objection to the state as the threat it poses to individual liberty. However, the key to Machan's criticism of Rothbard will again involve the idea that a 'morally legitimate' state would satisfy the anarchist's objections. Rothbard and Machan agree on what 'morally legitimate' entails here, that is, they both recognize the importance of individual liberty and the objections it poses to state coercion. "Governmental authority can be morally proper only when strictly limited to the protection and preservation of human rights" (Machan 1975, 146). Rothbard's point (this argument is also made by Randy Barnett) is that the services of conflict resolution and protection against violence can be provided more efficiently, and in greater concert with libertarian values, on an open market.

Machan then addresses himself to Rothbard specifically. Rothbard has argued that there is no such thing as a morally legitimate state, since all states rely for their power on coercion.

> [If] no one may morally initiate physical force against the person or property of another, then [even] limited government has built within it . . . impermissible aggression. . . . All governments, however limited they may be otherwise, commit . . . fundamental crimes against liberty and private property. (Rothbard 1972, 19).

Machan counters this by claiming that there is such a thing as a morally legitimate state, and that states of this sort are defensible on grounds that Rothbard should accept. "What I am saying against Rothbard is that it is in their interest and people are entitled to establish moral governments, ones that protect and preserve human rights (only)" (Machan 1975, 152).

Machan allows that, historically, states have contained the objectionable features Rothbard describes, although they ought not to be defined in this manner because they might conceivably be established without them.

> [W]e must acknowledge that Rothbard is here making something other than a historical claim about what governments have done. His contention is more general: there *could* not be a government that is not compulsory. . . . His reason is that any government must serve some given geographical area, which already renders it compulsory because some property owners who would prefer service from some other agency would not then be allowed to obtain it. But is this true? Would a government *have* to disallow secession? (Machan 1975, 148)

Machan's answer to this question is that the valid self-defense needs mentioned above might contractually rule out secession during specifically enumerated time periods, but that the government as legitimate hired agent of legitimate self-protection could be 'fired' if it proved unsatisfactory. Thus the government must exist to protect human rights, but need not be coercive in the manner objected to by Rothbard. Although "there must . . . exist a court of last resort," Machan writes,

> [I]t follows from the principles of human rights that action ought to be taken to institute their systematic protection and defense. If "government" is the concept best suited to designate such agencies, then it is morally justified for people to establish (hire) a proper government. It may be that those administering the laws will do a bad job, in which case one is morally obligated to alter or abolish (fire) those involved, provided terms are met for such disassociation. (Machan 1975, 151)

Puzzlingly, Machan allows for the possible efficiency of market-generated protection and arbitration services and shows a

considerable interest in the idea of non-coercive funding for government activities. If there were a free market in these services, and
they were funded non-coercively, that would indeed satisfy both
Machan's and Rothbard's conception of moral legitimacy, but it
would fail to be a "state" by our (or indeed most people's) definition. Machan's claims about implicit consent to just government
come so close to being anarchistic that the distinction is hard to
ascertain.

Moving from the original argument in his 1975 book to a later
clarification in a 1983 article, Machan says that the implicit consent to be governed need not imply consent to taxation, because
the services traditionally provided by governments that make governments desirable in the first place can be provided non-coercively. But this is *precisely* Rothbard's point: that services
traditionally provided by the state need not be so provided (and
that realizing this helps de-legitimize the state). Despite this development with regard to most services normally associated with the
state, Machan's primary worry seems to be the service of conflict
resolution, the only one he cannot imagine emerging on the market. "Unless something on the order of a court of *final* authority
exists, this [conflict resolution] is impossible in some cases [for
example when competing courts arrive at contrary decisions in a
given case]" (Machan 1983, 523). This claim is certainly true, but
rather than being the decisive argument against Rothbard (or anarchism generally), we shall view it as a challenge to Rothbard: can
he (or some other anarchist) present a plausible portrait of how
conflict resolution might occur without a state? It is precisely this
challenge that motivates Barnett, whose work will be discussed in
Chapter 4, as well as other work by Rothbard.

Machan's concern here *is* what I have characterized as a
"Hobbesian Fear." In addition, then, to examining various attempts
to meet the above challenge, we must note that what underlies the
challenge in the first place is a theory that will be questioned.

We may also see an opening for a criticism of the state in
Rasmussen and Den Uyl 2005. Rasmussen and Den Uyl say that
there "needs to be something that connects the ethical and the
political/legal orders" (85), and that is true. In this case, the idea is

to show that an "ethics of human flourishing supports an individual's right to liberty" and more specifically that "an ethics that conceives of human flourishing as the ultimate moral standard upholds
a political/legal order that sees protection of individual liberty as its
chief aim" (85). That's true also. Is the state compatible with this
vision? I don't think it is. Rasmussen and Den Uyl haven't said it is,
but they also haven't said it isn't, and this opens the door for com-
patibility between their vision of the nature of liberty and the sorts
of non-state-based social order proposed by Barnett, for example,
which will be examined in the next chapter.

Rasmussen and Den Uyl say, "The individual right to liberty
allows each person a sphere of freedom whereby self-directed activities can be exercised without being invaded by others. This translates socially into a principle of maximum compossible and equal
freedom for all" (90). Now it's clear enough that there will need to
be some kind of political/legal order to secure these rights. What
are its minimal specifications? We would need to have some sort of
established forum for resolving disputes or conflicts of interests
which may arise. We would like such a forum to be fair and unbi-
ased. That's "we" in the general sense—although a party to a pend-
ing dispute may at that time prefer a biased resolution process
(biased in his favor), as a general rule, it's in everyone's best interests to have the established procedures be known to be fair ones.
We might also desire some sort of enforcement or protection
agents. Given what Rasmussen and Den Uyl have, in my view, deci-
sively shown, we would like the fundamental principle governing
the other principles of adjudication to be the principle of liberty as
they have just explained. That is entirely consistent with the vision
of social order proposed by libertarian-anarchist theorists in the
next chapter.

Libertarianism Derived from Contractarian Theory

Of minimal-state theorists who take seriously the problem of justifying state coercion, Jan Narveson (in his 1988 book *The Libertarian
Idea*) comes closest to acknowledging his own difficulty in doing

so.[9] First, let us examine Narveson's conception of the state, after which it will be seen that if Narveson has any success in justifying it, it will be due to the sort of concern I have described as a Hobbesian Fear.

Narveson conceives of the state in the same terms as Nozick and Rothbard. Narveson describes the state as "a public with a government, and a government is a smallish subset of the public that has somehow acquired the power to rule, that is to say, to make people do the things it wants them to" (Narveson 1988, 208). Furthermore, the state claims "a monopoly on the use of force, in the specific sense that private uses of force must be authorized by it, whereas its own employments of force . . . are authorized *by itself*" (Narveson 1988, 208). Narveson thus understands the state in much the same way as do other minimal state theorists, and again, this is an understanding shared by anarchists.

However, Narveson is more skeptical than Nozick or Machan about how a power structure conceived this way can be reconciled with individual liberty, a value he shares with Nozick and Machan. "Authorities must be authorized, and in the end the only person who can 'authorize' anyone to do anything to you is *you*" (Narveson 1988, 214). This means that "the only authority a rational person acknowledges is authority that that person has good reason to accept" (Narveson 1988, 215). In addition to being the root of Narveson's skepticism about the legitimacy of state coercion, this sentiment is also why Narveson falls under the heading of contractarian. Like most libertarians, he uses the language of rights, but he does not actually generate libertarian principles from a conception of 'natural rights', but rather from the perspective of the contract theorist. The above caveat that a rational person will only authorize authority that he has "*good* reason to accept" echoes Locke's notion that the government needs

---

9. In the recent re-release of his 1988 book, Narveson disavows statism entirely. But others defend the minimal state by using Narveson's approach to libertarianism, so my remarks on the influential 1988 book remain germane.

to be authorized by consent of the governed, and then only when it remedies the inconveniences of the state of nature.

Narveson explicitly acknowledges David Gauthier's work in contractarian moral theory as the inspiration for his self-described contractarian approach to political principles. We have, Narveson argues, "good reason" to accept just enough authority to produce the minimal state, but not a more extensive state. The challenge from the anarchist is for Narveson to show whether we have good reason to accept even that much authority. But he warns the reader that he thinks this will be difficult to do, if it can be done at all (for example Narveson 1988, 223).

Narveson's approach to justifying the state, at least what seems to be his clearest strategy, is one of necessity. His discussion of the crucial role of conflict adjudication, that is, the role played by the courts, leads him to a similar final conclusion as Machan comes to, namely, that there has to be some mechanism for resolving conflicts between competing arbitration providers, and that having an ultimate authority of some sort might be found in 'the state'. However, Narveson does not say that this implies that the state is *necessary*. Having mentioned that the state in fact fills this role, he entertains the possibility of the "final arbitrator of disputes" being the result of some contractually pre-arranged mechanism that he says would be a natural development of any system of voluntary conflict resolution (Narveson 1988, 223). He does not actually endorse this conception either, but if the defense of the state rests on something like the claim that a naturally developing "final arbiter" will either not be forthcoming or not be efficient, then this will be another example of a Hobbesian Fear.

Shouldn't contracts that establish political obligation be unanimous? Can people have honest reasons for holding out on such contractual arrangements? David Schmidtz (1991) lays out the dilemma for us thus:

(1) If we know there are no honest holdouts, we do not need coercion. We can simply require unanimity as a precondition of the contract's validity. (2) If there are honest holdouts but we can tell them apart from others, we do not need coercion. We can require unanim-

ity among those who are not honest holdouts. (3) If we believe there
are honest holdouts but cannot identify them, then we may need
coercion, but in that case justifying coercion requires us to justify
using some as means to the ends of others. (Schmidtz 1991, 86–87)

But 'using some as means to the ends of others' is something that
Narveson, like Nozick and Machan, believes to be illegitimate.

Narveson argues that all rights are rights against other people,
that is, claims against one's liberty of action being interfered with
and not claims to specific things (Narveson 1988, 59). This distinction is sometimes made with the shorthand labels 'negative'
rights (for the former) and 'positive' rights (for the latter).
Therefore, he argues, there is no right to a state. Therefore, if the
state can be justified at all in Narveson's view, it will have to be on
grounds such as the non-feasibility of not having a state, for
instantce, that without one there could be no security of
covenants. This is actually familiar ground for someone who, like
Narveson, sees himself in the contractarian tradition, for the idea
of contractually organizing political units for the mutual benefit of
each of the parties to the contract is an idea found in Locke. But
when Narveson argues for the sort of state that would remedy the
"inconveniences of the state of nature," to use the Lockean phrase,
while not violating anyone's rights, he is describing a unit of social
organization that would lack the objectionable features of the state
which, in his view, are the defining characteristics of the state.
Defending this conception of a "morally legitimate state" misses
the point of the argument, but only a Hobbesian Fear could bridge
the gap between defending this and defending anything resem-
bling real states. This was essentially the outcome of Machan's
argument also, but unlike Machan, Narveson seems more sympathetic to the possibility that there is nothing further to be said on
behalf of the state.

4

Allaying the Hobbesian Fear

Having seen how various justifications of state coercion reduce to what I have described as a Hobbesian Fear, we must address this concern. Faced with the claim that the state is necessary for the enforcement of social cooperation—that without political authority we would be chaotically 'at each other's throats', we must examine various ways anarchist theorists attempt to answer this challenge.

Although philosophers have, by and large, tended to be quiescent about the Hobbesian Fear as a justification for state coercion, there have been several approaches to grappling with the problem it poses from other fields, specifically, law, economics, and decision theory (or game theory). One reason for this is that the Hobbesian Fear itself has been interpreted by these other fields. Before engaging in strictly philosophical considerations, it will be instructive to see what solutions theorists in these related fields have come up with to what is, after all, a matter of importance for political philosophy.

Of all political theories, we can separate out liberalism from other types of theories, and within the scope of liberal theory, we can separate out those theorists for whom individual liberty is the primary political concern, which we have been calling libertarian or classical liberal.[10] As we have seen, libertarian theorists give con-

---

10. It is currently fashionable for non-libertarian liberals to maintain that

ceptual priority to individual political liberty over other political values. We have seen that these theorists agree that political authority (the state) is something that requires justification, because the state is coercive by its very nature, and coercion is antithetical to human freedom and autonomy.

The disagreement surfaces when such a justification is attempted, for some libertarians argue that while the state must be limited in its scope to maximize human liberty, it is nevertheless neccssary, while other libertarians argue that the state is not only unjustified but in fact unnecessary. We have seen that the libertarian defenders of the state have a common concern at the heart of their defenses, which I have referred to as a Hobbesian Fear, because of its origin in Hobbes's argument in Chapters 13–14 of *Leviathan*. I now turn to attempts by libertarian anarchists to refute (or at least allay) the Hobbesian Fear, who by doing so hope to delegitimize the conception of political authority. These attempts proceed from the common ground that the anarchists share with the libertarian minimal-state theorists, namely (1) that states involve coercion; (2) that coercion is detrimental to human freedom; and (3) that human freedom is to receive first priority as a political value when constructing a political theory.

An Insight from Game Theory

It's commonplace in police dramas on TV and in the movies to see the detectives interrogate two people they suspect of committing a crime in separate rooms, in the hopes that one will implicate the other, which is what generally happens. Yet in dramas about organized crime, the suspects typically keep their mouths shut. What

---

libertarians 'aren't really' liberals, because the liberal tradition also includes more extensive, welfarist conceptions of the proper role of the state, and since libertarians deny these, they can't be liberals. See for example Freeman 2001, Spragens 1992a and 1992b. If we stipulatively define 'liberalism' as a welfarist theory, then it follows that libertarianism does not qualify. But on our broader understanding of liberalism (following Coleman's) as being a range of justificatory strategies or a set of values, libertarianism is a species of liberalism.

accounts for this distinction? As it happens, there is a large body of research into such situations.

Game theory is a cross-disciplinary family of theories about decision-making wherein options for each party are laid out in some form that permits study of outcomes. This can be used for descriptive or prescriptive study; that is, a decision theorist may study how parties actually act under certain conditions, or he may use the study to decide how parties should behave given their ends. Choices and outcomes are usually arranged in a matrix. One of the disputed areas of game theory is the degree of its accuracy regarding actual life, but we will observe that it is of some value even if we put restrictions on its applicability.[11]

What I have been referring to as the Hobbesian Fear has been interpreted by such theorists as John Rawls (1971), Nozick, and Gauthier as a representation of a situation similar to the familiar "Prisoner's Dilemma" in game theory (Luce and Raiffa, 1957).[12]

		B	
		cooperate	defect
	cooperate	A=3, B=3	A=0, B=5
A			
	defect	A=5, B=0	A=1, B=1

---

11. See, for example, Dyke 1985 for caveats about the applicability of the Prisoner's Dilemma to evolutionary situations. Dyke argues that the structure of the game can make it seem as though competition is taking place where it may not have been. For our purposes, however, we can proceed (with the caveat in mind) to take what we need from game theory, namely the conclusion that cooperation *may* (or could possibly) emerge spontaneously in a community of self-interested agents. We do not need Axelrod to have *proven* anything, only to have demonstrated a possible mechanism.

12. I mention these three as prominent philosophers who read Hobbes as presenting a Prisoner's Dilemma situation, but the decision-theory people have also made this connection. Michael Taylor, for instance, discussed it in his 1987 book, and Olson 1965 is frequently cited as an early occurrence of this way of looking at things. Although it is conventional to cite Luce and Raiffa 1957 as the

From A's point of view, if B is going to co-operate, A ought to choose defection, because this secures a higher payoff. On the other hand, if B is going to defect, A minimizes his (A's) penalty by choosing defection. In other words, it is rational for A to defect regardless of how B is expected to behave.[13] However, B is in precisely the same situation relative to A. If both defect, the payoff to both is less than if both had cooperated. So both parties, acting quite rationally, end up in a worse situation than they might have, for mutual cooperation would result in a higher payoff for both. In a Hobbesian argument, the sovereign is necessary to foster cooperation; that is, to make sure that 'players' (citizens) co-operate and therefore secure the more optimal 'payoff' (mutual security). On this model, authorizing state coercion is in one's best interest, and this *is* the justification.

Jean Hampton has elaborated on the interpretation of Hobbes's argument as a prisoner's dilemma situation.

> [T]he inhabitants of the state of nature would welcome the sovereign not only because he would be able to punish wrong-doers and solve prisoner's dilemmas but also because he could supply the external force necessary to discourage free riding in the production of collective goods. . . . the iterated [prisoner's dilemma] game argument is supposed to show the long-term rationality of performing the collectively rational act in those prisoner's dilemmas that are part of an

---

source for the Prisoner's Dilemma matrix, I learned from Axelrod that it "was invented in about 1950 by Merrill Flood and Melvin Drescher, and formalized by A.W. Tucker shortly thereafter (Axelrod 1984, 216).

13. We can explain rationality in somewhat more rigorous terms, as for example Coleman does here: "[T]he norms imposed by either a justified morality or political authority must weakly enhance each individual's utility, or, put slightly differently, each rational individual would agree to comply with the norms of a political morality only if ex ante each perceived compliance to be at least in his or her interest" (Coleman 1992, 20–21). Of course, further investigation into the nature of rationality would be a philosophically interesting pursuit (see for example Nozick 1993 and Nozick 2003). For our purposes, however, a common-sense understanding of rationality need only be supplemented by a standard game-theoretic definition such as the one Coleman uses.

indefinite series; but . . . [Hobbes has it that too many] people are likely to be shortsighted to make it rational for even farsighted people to trust that their partners will be true to their commitments. Thus, Hobbes's argument in *Leviathan* is that, in general, the inhabitants of the state of nature can solve their prisoner's dilemmas and free-rider problems *only* through the institution of the sovereign. (Hampton 1986, 134, emphasis added)

In other words, the coercion of the central political authority serves the useful purpose of fostering cooperation which might not otherwise arise. Looking at a Hobbesian Fear from a game-theoretic perspective, then, we shall next consider various possible responses to the challenge within this perspective.

One avenue for criticism here follows recent work in game theory research, notably that of Robert Axelrod, which seems to suggest that a Hobbesian Fear interpreted in this way rests on a mistake, that cooperation can and does evolve spontaneously, without a coercive system involving a monopoly of power such as a state. He presents his arguments for this in his book *The Evolution of Cooperation* (1984), as well as in some preliminary articles.[14] Axelrod developed a computer tournament to test the long term success of different strategies for winning at the prisoner's dilemma (where 'winning' is maximizing payoff not once, but over a long period). The outcome of several repetitions of the tournament was a clear victory for a strategy he calls "Tit for Tat." Tit-for-Tat attempts to foster cooperation while retaining a capacity to 'punish' when other 'players' refuse to cooperate. The method is deceptively simple: Cooperate on the first round, and then on each subsequent round do whatever the other player did in the previous round. Thus, higher payoffs were secured overall. No other strategy did as well. For instance, purely selfish 'players' who choose defection every round did not fare as well as 'players' who attempted to foster cooperation.

Naturally the winning strategy in a one-shot prisoner's dilemma is to defect. The point is that most of the life situations that are

---

14. For example, Axelrod and Hamilton 1981, 1390–96. I am grateful to Daniel Schmutter for bringing this to my attention.

thought to resemble a prisoner's dilemma are iterated (repeated) versions of the game, in which case the 'winning strategy' is to develop the sort of responsive cooperation that Axelrod describes.

Since Axelrod's influential work was first published, further experimentation has provided some interesting developments. More recently, Martin Nowak and Karl Sigmund (1993) have demonstrated greater success with a different strategy, one that outperforms tit-for-tat. It turns out that this new strategy, which they named "Pavlov," also indicates that responsive cooperation of the sort described by Axelrod is indeed the most robust.

> The Prisoner's Dilemma is the leading metaphor for the evolution of co-operative behaviour in populations of selfish agents, especially since the well-known computer tournaments of Axelrod and their application to biological communities. In Axelrod's simulations, the simple strategy of tit-for-tat did outstandingly well and subsequently became the major paradigm for reciprocal altruism. . . . Pavlov's success is based on two important advantages over tit-for-tat: it can correct occasional mistakes and exploit unconditional cooperators. (Nowak and Sigmund 1993, 56)

The Pavlov strategy is 'smarter' than Tit-for-Tat in that simple Tit-for-Tat cannot correct a 'misunderstanding' between 'players'. Since Tit-for-Tat involves simply repeating the other player's previous move, Tit-for-Tat is reactive. It tries to foster cooperation by initiating it, but thereafter is stuck with responding. So if the other player is 'dumb', that is, will not respond to Tit-for-Tat's attempt to cooperate, and defects, then Tit-for-Tat must defect. If both players are oriented towards Tit-for-Tat, but one makes a mistake, a cycle of mutual defection will result.

Pavlov can adjust based on previous favorable or unfavorable outcomes by cooperating after securing higher payoffs and defecting after lower payoffs (Nowak and Sigmund call this "win-stay, lose-shift"). Thus errors are corrected quickly. Although Pavlov is more robust than Tit-for-Tat, we notice that Axelrod's main point is not challenged, but in fact supported, by these new findings, namely, that responsive cooperation is an effective strategy for maximizing self-interest. If this is so, it is less clear that political authority is necessary to bring about cooperation.

Responsive cooperation means, more precisely, in both the cases of Tit-for-Tat and Pavlov, that the strategy has the properties Axelrod calls "nice, retaliatory, forgiving, and clear."

> [Tit-for-Tat's] niceness prevents it from getting into unnecessary trouble. Its retaliation discourages the other side from persisting whenever defection is tried. Its forgiveness helps restore mutual cooperation. And its clarity makes it intelligible to the other player, thereby eliciting long-term cooperation. (Axelrod 1984, 54)

Of course, Pavlov is also nice, retaliatory, forgiving, and clear, in addition to being smarter in the sense of being able to correct mistakes in the application of its attempts to foster mutual cooperation.[15]

In *Morals by Agreement*, Gauthier asserts that "contractarian" models of political cooperation *require* a sovereign for their efficacy. Yet he then argues that a contractarian *moral* (as opposed to political) theory, as a feature of rational-choice theory, would not require any more of an enforcer than one's own reason. One explanation for this seeming inconsistency is that, fearing a lapse in rationality, Gauthier believes that, in the political realm if not the moral, the sovereign enforcer is our only guarantor of security. While a Marxist such as Jon Elster (1982) might argue that *because* of lapses in individual rationality (as determined by whom?), the state ought to intervene (as a sort of collective rationality) to ensure that outcomes are the right ones, Gauthier is relying on rational choice theory to establish morality, and yet

---

15. We are being metaphorical when we describe Pavlov as "smarter," for the mechanism for correcting mistakes involves a mechanistic strategy. "The name [Pavlov] stems from the fact that the strategy embodies an almost reflex-like response to the payoff" (Nowak and Sigmund 1993, 56). Nevertheless, "our results suggest that cooperation based on win-stay, lose-shift may be more robust. The success of Pavlov-like behavior does not seem to be restricted to strategies, which only remember the last move" (Nowak and Sigmund 1993, 58).

wary of its consequences for social cooperation. Both of these sorts of critiques of rational-choice conceptions of social cooperation involve the fallacious assumption that since the model assumes perfect rationality, which would not obtain, there must be a problem with adopting the model. Actually, it is not a perfect-rationality model that is being assumed at all, but an imperfect-rationality model. The claim is merely that people are trying to do what is thought to be best for them. Obviously, sometimes people make mistakes, but they are nevertheless trying to work out the best way to accomplish their ends.

We must keep in mind what the Prisoner's Dilemma is supposed to do. It is supposed to show how individual rationality, that is, individuals doing their best to achieve their own ends, can lead to a less-than-optimal situation, as the game theory analysis clearly shows. The dominant strategy when playing the game is obviously to defect, and since both players are in the same position, the dominant strategy for both of them is to defect, yet the double-defect box in the matrix is less than optimal. Of course, the both-not-defect box is better for both. The question arises because defecting is the dominant strategy only if you play the game just once. It is not the dominant strategy, the research shows, if you play the game in series, that is, over and over again. It turns out in that case that the most effective strategy is responsive cooperation of the sort that Tit-for-Tat and Pavlov exhibit.

The question is, then: Is life 'like' the one-shot dilemma or 'like' the iterated dilemma? Clearly, *some* situations seem to resemble the iterated dilemma. In terms of relevant applications of the game theory model, there is stronger resemblance to the iterated game, for instance in dealings in the business community. Companies and businessmen have trade relations over a period of time, not just once. Anything like the trade relations of the business community is more appropriately modeled on the iterated game, not the one-shot dilemma. International relations (trade agreements, border disputes, and so forth), for example, fit this description. If the dominant strategy already is cooperation, then coercion is not necessary. The social cooperation that is deemed necessary by minimal-statism is the sort of cooperation that would have to develop naturally if it is the sort of cooperation that is represented by the iterated dilemma. (People are sometimes not rational, but this alone cannot be the justification for state coercion unless we are to have philosopher-kings.) Since the guidelines for the prisoner's dilemma dictate no communication between the players, one might also argue that all the prisoner's dilemma shows is that people make less-than-optimal decisions when under circumstances of insufficient information.

Citing historical work by a sociologist, Tony Ashworth, Axelrod interprets a real-world example of spontaneously developing cooperation in terms of his game-theoretical framework. The example is from the trench warfare of World War I, where a peculiar phenomenon was observed by visiting British officers: British and German troops would show considerable restraint in not shooting each other across the trench lines, a phenomenon referred to by disgusted British officers as "live and let live."

> While Ashworth does not put it this way, the historical situation in the quiet sectors along the western front was an iterated Prisoner's Dilemma. . . . At any given moment it was prudent to shoot to kill whether the enemy did so or not. What made trench warfare so different from most other combat was that the same small units faced each other in immobile sectors for extended periods of time. (Axelrod 1984, 75–77)

Conceiving of this as a prisoner's dilemma situation, it is clear that the parties had adopted the Tit for Tat strategy, that is, neither would be the first to defect, but would respond reciprocally if provoked by a defection. This produced the more beneficial outcome than the alternative of shooting to kill whenever anyone was in range. Although these micro-truces were the optimal outcome for the troops involved, they were naturally not optimal for the political leaders who were trying to conduct a war. The stability of 'live and let live' in the trenches was eroded by strategic change on the part of the leadership, specifically, the development of raiding parties, which could be controlled from central command locations. The breakdown of cooperation was not due to instability of the strategy.

> Cooperation got a foothold through exploratory actions at the local
> level, was able to sustain itself because of the duration of contact
> between small units facing each other, and was eventually undermined
> when these small units lost their freedom of action. (Axelrod 1984, 83)

> Although the cooperative strategy evolved spontaneously, it was not a
> blind or random process. Rather, it involved the participants in the sit-
> uation understanding that mutual cooperation would be more advan-
> tageous, and learning how this cooperation depended partly upon
> restraint, and partly upon willingness to reciprocate when provoked
> (Axelrod 1984, 84).

Axelrod goes on to argue that, in addition to bearing out the
predictions of his theory of cooperation, this example adds a new
element to the theory—the emergence of an ethics based on the
participants coming to recognize and value the mutual cooperation. This addition is based on other historical evidence of apolo-
gies being issued across the trenches when artillery was fired
without the knowledge of the infantry.

> The self-reinforcement of these mutual behavioral patterns was not
> only in terms of the interacting strategies of the players, but also in
> terms of their perceptions of the meanings of the outcomes. In
> abstract terms, the point is that not only did preferences affect behav-
> ior and outcomes, but behavior and outcomes also affected prefer-
> ences. (Axelrod 1984, 85)

The possibility of developing ethics from the stability of the cooperative strategy, not just social order, is a ramification that further
undercuts Gauthier's concerns about perfect rationality. Gauthier
argues that rational choice produces morality but not necessarily
social order; Axelrod shows that even imperfect rationality will
develop social order and might produce morality. In any event,
whether or not an ethics can emerge spontaneously, the game-theory interpretation of the Hobbesian Fear as a justification for *political* authority is undermined by experimental research in game
theory itself.

Another approach, however, to criticizing a Hobbesian Fear
within a game-theoretic perspective is to question the accuracy of

what it portrays. There are other historical counter-examples to what the argument claims would be the result of a lack of political authority. First of all we might keep in mind the 'international relations' objection to the claim. Upon reflection, one realizes that individual nation-states *are* in the Hobbesian state of nature relative to each other, there being no world government, and yet the world is *not* in a perpetual state of war of all against all. This was pointed out by critics as early as Locke, yet the Hobbesian argument retains its traction. On a strict application of Hobbes's definition of war, states of war do exist between some countries that aren't actually fighting, but it is not the case that the whole world is in such a condition. More often than not, countries work out Tit-for-Tat-like or Pavlov-like cooperative strategies.

Michael Taylor makes this point in his 1987 book *The Possibility of Cooperation*. Although Hobbes did not apply to the international "state of nature" the analysis he made of the domestic one, Taylor argues, "there is no reason in principle why such an application should not be made. . . . [So] the possibility of conditional cooperation amongst states in the absence of [a] supranational state has been taken more seriously in the last few years" regarding the possibility of cooperation generally (Taylor 1987, 166). Barnett also makes this observation: "The argument that we need court systems with geography-based jurisdictional monopolies does not stop at the border of a nation-state. Any such argument suggests the need for a single world court system. . . . After all, the logic of the argument against a competitive legal order applies with equal force to autonomous nations" (Barnett 1986, 42).

While evaluating Hobbes's premises, we must also put a critical eye to the distinction between being egoistic—that is, being self-interested—and being anti-social. A Hobbesian Fear depends on people being anti-social, not just self-interested, in order to necessitate the Leviathan, but all Hobbes can establish is that people are self-interested. He cannot show what he needs to show merely by pointing out the fact of human self-interest, particularly in the face of Axelrod's findings that cooperation *is* the dominant social strategy for self-interested agents.

In this regard, it is worth noting Rothbard's claim (1978) that although it is true that the society he has in mind needs, in order to function, a certain amount of human disposition to get along ("not hell-bent on destroying their neighbors"), this is so only as much as any society needs these things, so they must be pretty reasonable assumptions. All he wants to presuppose are things that any society, statist or anarchist, must presuppose. There would no doubt be socially emergent conceptions of contract law and so on, as there was in Europe and England before the state's consolidation of these functions, "but the idea that the state is needed to *make* law is as much a myth as that the state is needed to supply postal . . . services" (Rothbard 1978, 206).

Another example of social cooperation being an evolved mechanism is found in Hayek. Hayek argues in *Law, Legislation, and Liberty* that the English common law is actually an example of this spontaneously-evolved cooperative enterprise. The common law is essentially an enshrining of evolved practices which enable peaceable dispute resolution, and not the product of legislation, deliberate planning. Rules of law arise through repeated human interaction. Patterns, and expectations of adherence to patterns, emerge. Juries are asked to apply the commonly accepted rules for settling disputes which, in principle anyway, embody the general consensus about what is fair as revealed in actual practice. Judges are expected to follow precedent when applying principles in their rulings. The common law is both stable and vital; that is, it contains elements that carry on across time, enabling people to have reasonable expectations about the future, and also elements that enable the procedures and policies to adapt to changing times. Without being the product of any intentional design, it nevertheless comes into being and produces order.

How Polycentric Legal Theory Benefits from Axelrod's Work

Rothbard and Barnett both suggest hypothetical scenarios of how non-monopolistic and non-coercively financed legal systems would operate. Their claims about the feasibility of these systems depend on the falsehood of the Hobbesian Fear. What is interesting is that the Axelrod conclusions make the anarchist legal theory more sensible. One might be tempted to dismiss the Hobbesian Fear altogether, but a stronger argument can be made by using Axelrod's work to raise questions about the Hobbesian Fear. Yet if the Hobbesian Fear is the ultimate point of contention between minimal-state libertarians and anarchist libertarians, then applying the lessons of Axelrod's work to minimal-state theory will show that it is mistaken: the state is not *necessary* for social order. Although laboratory experiments of the sort performed by Axelrod and Nowak and Sigmund cannot tell us how societies actually developed cooperative structures, they can tell us what is possible. It is possible for cooperative structures to emerge spontaneously, without political authority and coercion. This possibility is sufficient to render the Hobbesian Fear less worrisome and the anarchist claims more plausible.

According to the game theory research, cooperation is the social strategy that produces the most favorable outcome in the long run, even if everyone is primarily concerned with self-interest. Libertarian minimal statists argue that the state, although undesirable in general, is necessary to ensure the minimal social cooperation necessary for society's existence. Libertarian anarchists argue that schemes of conflict resolution and security provision could arise without coercion because the minimal level of social cooperation postulated by the minimal-state theorists is the level that would arise spontaneously as a result of people pursuing their self-interest. What seems to be an insoluble hypothetical dispute about the necessity of the state for the provision of cooperation can be mediated, I think, by looking at what the game-theory research suggests. If the minimal-state libertarians all have at their base something like the Hobbesian Fear about the results of a lack of political authority, and the Hobbesian Fear can be brought into question, then the anarchist libertarians will have a much stronger position. Let us now turn to an examination of how the game-theory research speaks to the concerns of the minimal-statists and supports the arguments of the anarchists.

We have seen that Nozick argues that the dominant protective agency can prohibit private enforcement of justice because allowing it entails risks that threaten the security of its clients. Since one has a right, on Nozick's account, to prevent others from engaging in risky behavior that could decrease one's security, one has a right to authorize another to do this on one's behalf. But does it follow from this that one has a right to forbid others from joining other protective associations? Nozick himself brings up this question (Nozick 1974, 121) in order to respond to it in advance. His answer seems to undermine his own argument, however.

> We have found a distinction, which appears to be theoretically significant, that distinguishes a protective agency's forbidding others from using unreliable or unfair procedures to exact justice on its clients from other prohibitions—such as forbidding others to form another protective agency—which might be thought to be allowable if the first is. . . . [But we] have rebutted the charge we imagined earlier that our argument fails because it "proves" too much, in that it provides a rationale not only for the permissible rise of a dominant protective association, but also for this association's forcing someone not to take his patronage elsewhere or for some person's forcing others not to join any association. *Our argument provides no rationale for the latter actions and cannot be used to defend them.* (Nozick 1974, 129, emphasis added)

If the argument does not provide a justification for the dominant protective association forbidding individuals from opting out, then Nozick has no argument for the state beyond that one *could* arise without violating anyone's rights. However, he views this development as more than simply a logical possibility. He argues that the minimal state is actually justified as a matter of collective decision making. As we have seen, Nozick argues that the dominant protective agency is justified in prohibiting people from seeking other means of settling disputes on the grounds that it would be too risky to permit such actions. Although he describes the fair (meaning non-rights violating) procedures which would most likely be followed by the dominant protective agency, he must believe that no competitive set of such agencies could be fair and feasible. In fact, his dismissal of Rothbard's (1970) proposal for just such a system indicates this:

> Rothbard imagines that somehow, in a free society, "the decision of any two courts will be considered binding, i.e., will be the point at which the court will be able to take action against the party adjudged guilty." . . . Why is anyone who has not in advance agreed to such a two-court principle be bound by it? Does Rothbard mean anything other than that he expects agencies won't act until two independent courts (the second being an appeals court) have agreed? (Nozick 1974, 343)

In fact, it is precisely Rothbard's point that the sensible thing to expect is that the agencies would act only after the adjudicating was complete, and that a likely arrangement would be one in which the various courts one might be a 'client' of would have pre-arranged means for resolving *their* disputes. Do we have any reason to think the companies would seek this (co-operative) type of a solution, rather than resorting to violent conflict? According to Axelrod (or more precisely, Ashworth), we do have some reason for thinking this is plausible. Nozick can only rule out this possibility by appeal to a Hobbesian Fear. But here we have a clear example of how the insights from game theory support the position of an anarchist criticism of Nozick, specifically the one found in Randy Barnett's work, most recently his 1998 book *The Structure of Liberty*.

In opposition to Nozick's claim that a legal order would of necessity—as a matter of market efficiency—be monopolistic, Randy Barnett's recent work on polycentric legal systems poses a theoretical challenge to this sort of minimalism. Even if we interpret Nozick as saying merely that his minimal state is *acceptable* under his set of constraints (rather than necessary for whatever reason), Barnett argues, we still have no reason to accept its monopolistic status; for if we could devise one that did more of what we expect from a legal system, in a more efficient manner, and without damaging other commodities valued by Nozick such as the ideal of liberty, then we could have social order without coercion.

Legal systems in our society involve monopolistic institutions, such as a court system and a police force. Unsurprisingly, these tend to be inefficient and susceptible to corruption, and, more to the point, they are coercive. Barnett thinks that a legal order need not involve any monopolistic institutions, and that doing without them better promotes justice, and without sacrificing individual liberty. ("Pursuing Justice in a Free Society," *Criminal Justice Ethics* IV, part 2 (1986), and more recently, *The Structure of Liberty* (1998)). According to Barnett, Nozick's "invisible-hand" justification for the state does not match his own values as well as it could, because his conception of a legal system, that is, a system providing for redress of grievances and torts, does not need to be monopolistic or coercive.

Part of the confusion that often arises in this area (although not in Nozick) is due to a confusion about what have come to be called positive and negative rights. Following Isaiah Berlin, we might distinguish between welfare-rights (or positive rights) and freedom-rights (or negative rights). The 'right to free speech' is an example of the latter; the 'right to decent housing' is an example of the former. In a given context, there is no intrinsic conceptual problem with positive rights. For example, one has a right to go backstage at a concert if one has received a proper backstage pass. But out of the context of a guest list, there is no such thing as a natural right to go backstage. From the perspective of Nozick or Narveson, free from any context, there actually can be no positive rights.

To assert a positive right is to create an obligation on someone else to provide the thing claimed. This obligation cannot be natural, it can only be contractual. Narveson, at any rate, is quite clear about this distinction and what each category would have to entail. He suggests that one consider the obligations said to follow from the different claims. What would it mean for the relation to be natural? If I had an obligation to provide the thing to one person, do I also have an obligation to provide it to all? Or just to everyone in my neighborhood? If not, why not? If the person does have a right to the thing, why is the corresponding obligation on me and not someone else? There is no end to the theoretical difficulty with asserting natural positive rights.

Negative rights, on this view, pose no such difficulties. To assert a negative right is merely to rule out interference in my action (*prima facie*). What would justify the interference? One answer would be, the extent to which my action would interfere with another's legitimate rights (which is the answer J. S. Mill is famous for). But a logically consistent conception of rights would rule this out. For example, any number of people exercising their Lockean "right to their own person and labor" would not conflict with each other's doing so. Hence this might be legitimately asserted as a right. Hillel Steiner refers to a set of such non-conflicting rights as "co-possible" or "compossible" rights. Such a set is one in which "it is logically impossible for one individual's exercise of his rights within that set to constitute an interference with another individual's exercise of his rights within that same set" (Steiner 1977, 769). Barnett argues that the legal system of any rights-oriented society must, as a "logical requirement," recognize only compossible rights (Barnett 1985, 53). Otherwise conflicts will have to be settled by appeal to something other than rights.

The usual libertarian approaches to property rights do not conflict with this, because property rights in that sense, while clearly positive, are part of the context of the society that enforces them. This also does not require a monopolistic coercive authority, that is, a state; only a society that in fact recognizes the practicality of recognizing property rights. Can this kind of society exist without the state? Rothbard and other theorists think so.

Rothbard and David Friedman have argued that the development of the common law and the merchant societies in medieval England and Ireland, along with similar developments in Iceland, demonstrated the manner in which social cooperation with regard to the institution of conflict resolution emerged spontaneously. Let us first turn to Friedman's analysis of Iceland.

> In medieval Iceland all law was civil. The victim was responsible for enforcing his claim, individually or with the assistance of others.... Because the Icelandic system relied entirely on private enforcement, it can be seen as a system of civil law expanded to include what we think of as criminal offenses.... the typical settlement was a cash payment to

the victim or his heirs. The alternative, if you lost your case, was out-lawry [where outlaws are defined as those who may be killed without legal consequence if they do not leave Iceland]. (Friedman 1989, 204)

After noticing that this arrangement was remarkably stable for around three hundred years, Friedman points out what he sees as a key point: that the enforcement of law in this setting did not depend on "an organization with special rights beyond those possessed by all individuals" (Friedman 1989, 208). Modern conceptions of private agencies of enforcement and competing, independent courts are the same principles, he argues, "applied to a much larger and more complicated society" (Friedman 1989, 208).

In *Power and Market* (1970), one of Rothbard's arguments against a state-based conception of property rights is that the principles operative in a free society in the first place are ones that provide a theory of property rights already; namely, self-ownership and ownership of resources transformed by one's labor. This is obviously Lockean, and Rothbard thinks that this Lockean conception means that the state is not necessary to define or allocate property rights. In any case, it means that minimal-state libertarians should not be relying on the premise that the state is needed to define property rights.

Rothbard suggests we re-examine the Hobbesian Fear with irreverence:

> Suppose, for example, that we were all suddenly dropped down on the earth *de novo* and that we were all then confronted with the question of what societal arrangements to adopt. And suppose then that some-one suggested: "We are all bound to suffer from those of us who wish to aggress against their fellow men. Let us then solve this problem of crime by handing all of our weapons to the Jones family, over there, by giving all of our ultimate power to settle disputes to that family. In that way, with their monopoly of coercion and of ultimate decision making, the Jones family will be able to protect us from each other." I submit that this proposal would get very short shrift, except perhaps from the Jones family themselves. And yet this is precisely the common argument for the existence of the state. (Rothbard 1978, 195)

Reading 'the sovereign' for "the Jones family," we see Rothbard's parody of Hobbes's argument here. But then the question remains which societal arrangements to adopt. Rothbard suggests that we adopt not *a* system of conflict resolution, but several.[16] We have already seen, for example in Machan, that any such suggestion will be challenged by the need to have a final arbiter of disputes if chaos is to be avoided. But Rothbard's response, that a spontaneously arising competitive legal system would be stable, is more plausible in light of Axelrod's conclusion that cooperation is the dominant strategy.

Rothbard's arguments for non-monopolistic, non-coercively funded legal institutions are elaborated on by Randy Barnett. To understand fully the manner in which Barnett's theory is an effective criticism of minimal-statism, we must see how he wants to re-evaluate the concept of a legal system, and move away from the usual 'punishment versus deterrence' arguments towards a restitutive conception of criminal justice. The arcane statutes that are supposed to regulate conduct, such as fire codes, are removed from one's experience to a certain degree. Fear of personal reprisal is never so removed. If a nightclub owner, for example, is told by an inspector that he must comply with certain statutes, the owner fears being fined for non-compliance. The worst-case scenario for him is facing charges such as involuntary manslaughter or culpable negligence. If the nightclub owner faced a system of strict liability, he would have to worry about multiple lawsuits for his actions from the many wronged patrons (or their survivors), as opposed to the one charge for the code violation. Strict liability can be defined as the rule governing cases where "the victim must show that 1. She has suffered a compensable loss. 2. The injurer acted. 3. The injurer's conduct caused the

---

16. "Consistent with this distinction the phrase 'legal order' will be used when speaking of the entire legal structure [of even an anarchist society] and the phrase 'legal system' when speaking of one court or other dispute resolution system within the larger order. A nonmonopolistic legal order, then, would be likely to consist of several legal systems" (Barnett 1986, 51).

loss she [the victim] seeks to have repaired" (Coleman 1992, 212).[17]

Strict liability, then, would create a much more real incentive to (in this case) have well-lit exits, or whatever. This is the sort of example Barnett uses to illustrate a process by which a statist legal system is actually less efficient at promoting justice. The state's enforcement pre-empts or mitigates the element of personal reprisal that might make a more tangible deterrent. This also brings us back to the problem of simple punishment versus restitution. If the above-mentioned nightclub owner is found guilty of culpable negligence and is sentenced to seven years in prison, this does not increase the utility of the families of the patrons who could not find the exits. Since nothing the owner could do would bring back the dead, some form of restitution is an efficient means of producing benefit for the next of kin. Jules Coleman explains:

> Compensating a victim involves making him whole in more than one way. It involves the rather complex idea of leaving him indifferent in welfare or utility terms between his position ex ante and ex post. It expresses as well the morally complex and important idea that the liberal conception of autonomy is not extinguished by the misfortune or injustice of injury and accident. Compensating resources are awarded to put the victim back to where he would have been had the accident not occurred, both morally and otherwise. Resources are provided for his use in the light of his projects, plans and goals, projects and goals that may have been altered by his injury, but ones which are nevertheless his to formulate and to execute. . . . [This conception of justice] sustains norms that encourage coordination and sustain important social institutions. These norms provide part of the stable

---

17. The contrast here is with what is known as fault liability. Coleman says that if a case is governed by fault liability, the victim must show that in addition to the three conditions of strict liability, that the injurer was at fault in acting (Coleman 1992, 212). Under a fault liability conception, I can only be held responsible for negative consequences of actions defined to be bad, whereas under strict liability I can be held responsible for negative consequences of any action. Clearly strict liability provides me with a greater incentive to act in a reasonable way.

framework within which free and equal individuals pursue the projects and goals they believe contribute to their well-being. (Coleman 1992, 438–39)

In other words, the restitutive 'making whole' is a figurative expression which refers to *some* direct benefit to the victim which makes him better off. If the loss is monetary, obviously the restitution is easily calculable. If not, some more complicated scheme would have to be agreed upon by the various enforcement agencies.

Barnett's point is that adopting a strict liability conception of legal responsibility and a restitutive approach to punishment makes non-monopolistic systems of conflict resolution feasible. This makes sense as long as there is sufficient social cooperation to allow the different enforcement agencies to develop strategies of coexistence that would not be chaotic. But according to Axelrod and the others, this condition can be met.

Since both retributive and deterrence goals are served by restitution, either sort of theorist would do well to endorse a restitutive conception of punishment. But this conception does not *require* a monopolistic enforcer such as the state, unless we accept a justification for the state that is based on a Hobbesian Fear. So the question that remains is how a non-monopolistic legal system could function, and whether the game-theory conclusions about cooperation make these scenarios more plausible.

Barnett and Rothbard describe similar schemes whereby conflict resolution, conceived of as another service more efficiently provided on a market, is provided without a coercive authority, that is, by consent. The state, even when organized by majority rule, has free reign to violate the consent of the minority. (Locke suggests in Section 98 of the *Second Treatise* that unanimity *is* better than majoritarianism, but since it is seldom obtained, we must settle for majority rule. This too is another example of a Hobbesian Fear.)

Barnett applies the traditional conception of 'the problem of the commons' to crime prevention. The problem of the commons is the inefficient use of resources which arises because there is no exclusion or imperfect exclusion of some users from assets considered to be common property. Barnett argues that in a statist society, parks, streets, and other public spaces are viewed as being held in common, and this has an adverse effect on crime prevention, for two main reasons: there is no right to exclude, since these assets are considered to 'belong to everybody', and little incentive to commit resources to assist in crime prevention, since it is thought of as having already been paid for (Barnett 1986, 32).

> When property rights are ill-defined, misallocations of resources will occur. If a particular resource is held in common . . . then no person has the right to exclude others from using the resource. Without the right to exclude, it is unlikely that the benefits accruing to persons who privately invest in the care or improvement of a resource will exceed the costs of their efforts. . . . For this reason, commonly held resources are typically overused and undermaintained. (Barnett 1986, 31)

Barnett sees law-enforcement as, at least partly, a 'commons' problem. He argues that this has adverse effects on the state's ability to prevent crime. A statist society that values freedom, for example, a libertarian state, has to deny government police agencies the rights to regulate public property that private property owners enjoy. "Yet steps taken to protect society from the government also serve to make citizens more vulnerable to criminally inclined persons by providing such persons with a greater opportunity for a safe haven on the public streets" (Barnett 1986, 33). Barnett argues that the only way to resolve this dilemma while preserving freedom is to adopt a robust approach to property rights and to permit competing agencies to provide adjudication and enforcement services.

Barnett argues (as does Rothbard), that protective agencies have market-generated incentives to respect the "rights of the accused," incentives monopoly police agents lack; and also that competing "conflict resolution specialists" (judges) have market incentives to be fair in their decision making, incentives that monopoly judges lack. According to Barnett, this will mean that violations of (compossible) rights will have an avenue for redress without a coercive state where such avenue would not in the process violate the rights of the innocent, particularly by not being coercively funded.

Rothbard favors a form of indenture to imprisonment (even privatized imprisonment) because it better promotes the conception of restitution to the victim. The number of people for whom imprisonment is necessary to prevent repeat offenses without enforceable restitution (for example psychotic axe murderers) is pretty small. So there might be one or two private houses of imprisonment for what he calls "nonactionable tortfeasors," which would have the usual market checks against wrongful imprisonment. The rest of the criminal punishments are done through a restitutive system, the bottom line of which is indenture.

Bruce Benson makes a similar point when he argues that "The arguments for public provision of law and its enforcement are largely 'market failure' arguments, which imply that the private sector will not efficiently produce law and order. The implicit assumption underlying [this] . . . is that when the market fails, government can do better" (Benson 1990, 271). Free riding is possible, he says, but "we can expect that contractual arrangements will evolve that exclude free riders from the benefits of reciprocally organized protection arrangements, as they did in [for example] Anglo-Saxon England" (Benson 1990, 276).

This is a crucial observation by Benson: arguments for the justification of the state based on an economist's conception of the market's failure to provide conflict resolution or rights protection (or any other service, for that matter) assume that governments will provide the service flawlessly and without corruption. Rothbard has assailed this pattern of argumentation: "it is illegitimate to compare the merits of anarchism and statism by starting with the present system as the implicit given and then critically examining only the anarchist alternative" (Rothbard 1978, 195). Do governments in the real world provide services efficiently and uncorruptly, or are there moral and pragmatic difficulties with the manner in which governments operate? One cannot use the necessity of the state as a premise in order to reach it as a conclusion.

So what actually are the 'checks and balances' that Rothbard, Barnett, and Benson think will make a polycentric legal system work? Private courts would, on this model, depend for their success on a reputation for fairness and objectivity. What machinery ensures this? The normal operation of a system like this provides a finite number of scenarios. If Jones and Smith are in dispute, and both are clients of Adjudication Service A, or Court A, then both will have previously agreed to be bound by its decision. If Smith is a client of Court A, and Jones is a client of court B, then there are more possibilities (although still finite). In this case, if both Court A and Court B agree that Smith's case (or Jones's) is the more meritorious, then both parties will have previously agreed to respect the result. The troubling scenario is the one in which Court A finds for Smith and Court B finds for Jones (or the other way around, I suppose). But as long as Court A and Court B have a prior arrangement to have *their* disputes resolved by some third adjudication service, the situation might not be so troubling after all. In this case, the decision of two of the three adjudicators makes the decision. There is still room for trouble. Suppose Smith, upon the decision of Courts B and C that he is in the wrong, decides to violate his prior agreement to abide by such a decision. What mechanisms could exist to respond to this? One possibility is that Smith would be dropped from the protection service that is part of agreeing to all this. The fear of losing his protective service would operate as an incentive on Smith to 'behave'. Being dropped from a protective service in this manner would have the same effect on his ability to engage other protective services as failure to make car payments has on obtaining credit from other lenders. Cooperation in this respect at least can be accounted for by self-interest, as Axelrod suggests. Repeatedly reneging on agreements such as these would be like defecting in an iterated prisoner's dilemma: an unsuccessful strategy. Indeed, Barnett makes a passing reference to Axelrod in the following passage, in which he (Barnett) offers his answer to the fear that the competing systems would war with each other:

> Extended conflict between competing court systems is quite unlikely. It is simply not in the interest of repeat players (and most of their clients) to attempt to obtain short-run gains at the cost of long-run

conflict. Where they have the opportunity to cooperate, in even the most intense conflicts—warfare, for example—participants tend to evolve a "live and let live" philosophy [Barnett's footnote here is to Axelrod] . . . How much greater the incentive to cooperate would be if competing judicial services did not have access to a steady stream of coercively obtained revenue—that is, by taxation. (Barnett 1986, 41)

This is Barnett's only mention of Axelrod but, clearly, the more one looks into Axelrod's work on cooperation,[18] the more plausible Barnett's claims about cooperation become.

Nor is free riding a substantial worry, according to Schmidtz:

People would not be able to free ride on the general deterrent effect of other people's contributions for contract enforcement because the deterrent effect would be relevant only to those who have paid to become subject to it. If Jane's contract makes no arrangements for its own enforcement, the upshot is not that the level of enforcement suffers a light drop but rather that the *scope* of enforcement is not extended to protect Jane; Jane's contract is not enforced. . . . The paradigmatically emergent justification for [the use of force involved in enforcement of mutually agreeable contracts] is based on actual consent. (Schmidtz 1991, 98–99)

While Rothbard and Barnett merely theorize that mechanisms like this would maintain social order, there is actually historical precedent for this sort of conflict resolution system. According to Anderson and Hill (1979 and 2004), during the settlement period in the American west, before federal power had extended into the territories, conflicts were resolved by exactly the sort of 'private

---

18. Also Taylor 1987; Nowak and Sigmund 1993; Anderson and Hill 1979. The point is that the game-theory research on the evolution of cooperation plays a more useful role in supporting the arguments for polycentric legal systems than even the proponents of those arguments realize. When first reading Rothbard or Barnett on competing agencies of adjudication or enforcement, one's intuitions will either accept the claims as sensible or generate objections about whether such systems would break down. The game-theory research can help Barnett and Rothbard persuade readers of the latter disposition.

courts' Rothbard and Barnett envision: "[A]rbitration came from a 'private court' consisting of 'three disinterested men,' one chose by each side and a third chosen by the two. . . . Competition rather than coercion insured justice" (Anderson and Hill 1979, 25). The wagon trains, mining camps, and frontier towns apparently maintained a considerable degree of social order and respect for persons and property prior to the arrival of federal power. Indeed, in each case Anderson and Hill cite, social order actually decreased after monopolistic justice arrived.

> [I]n five of the major cattle towns (Abilene, Ellsworth, Wichita, Dodge City, and Caldwell) for the years from 1870 to 1885, only 45 homicides were reported—an average of 1.5 per cattle-trading season. In Abilene, supposedly one of the wildest of the cow towns, "nobody was killed in 1869 or 1870." . . . Only two towns, Ellsworth in 1873 and Dodge City in 1876, ever had five killings in any one year. (Anderson and Hill 1979, 14)

Surprising statistics like these suggest that the popular image of the 'shoot-em-up' wild-west lifestyle is largely without basis in fact. In addition, the statistics are less surprising in light of what we learned from Axelrod about the stability of spontaneously-evolved social cooperation when the disposition to respond reciprocally to 'defection' is generally understood. Anderson and Hill's historical findings, like Benson's, fit Axelrod's theoretical framework neatly.

Anderson and Hill suggest that social order was maintained in 'anarchistic' ways partially because of certain points of "commonality that exist . . . in the minds of the participants in some social situation" (Anderson and Hill 1979, 12). Without making extravagant claims about human nature, it seems sensible that this sort of general agreement is what facilitates social cooperation in the absence of a political enforcement mechanism. "Thus when a miner argued that a placer claim was his because he 'was there first', that claim carried more weight than if he claimed it simply because he was most powerful" (Anderson and Hill 1979, 12).

This conception of points of general agreement would account for many examples of non-monopolistic, consensual means of conflict resolution: the development of the English Common Law and

Law Merchant prior to the consolidation of these by the crown, the Middle Eastern merchant associations, and the civil law in medieval Iceland and Ireland. The history of the development of law shows that socially emergent conceptions of legal principles, for example, that one is innocent until proven guilty, occur prior to their adoption by the political authority.

Benson explains why this is the case:

> The attributes of customary legal systems include an emphasis on individual rights because legal duty requires voluntary cooperation of individuals through reciprocal arrangements. Such laws and their accompanying enforcement facilitate cooperative interaction by creating strong incentives to avoid violent forms of dispute resolution. . . . Thus, the law provides for restitution to victims arrived at through clearly designed participatory adjudication procedures, in order to both provide incentives to pursue prosecution and to quell victims' desires for revenge. Strong incentives for both offenders and victims to submit to adjudication as a consequence of social ostracism or boycott sanctions, and legal change occurs through spontaneous evolution of customs and norms. (Benson 1990, 36)

Benson's hypothesis explains both why the customary law, developed 'from the bottom up', is typically accepted by most people and why law imposed from the top down frequently is not. Benson arrives at this conclusion after noticing the extent to which Anglo-Saxon common law depended upon a conception of legal duty not rooted in imposed political power but in mutual benefit. Again, the insights we glean from Axelrod's findings make these arguments more plausible.

The idea of a system of conflict resolution based on mutual benefit and thus popular acceptance seems like a simple one, so we should not be surprised to discover that the legal systems of so-called 'primitive societies' frequently are built on such principles. Besides surveying the development of the common law in Europe, Benson also cites Leopold Pospisil's study of the legal system of New Guinea's Kapauku culture, which turns out to bear a striking similarity to the systems suggested by Rothbard and Barnett. Their culture provides for

1) primary rules characterized by a predominant concern for *individual rights and private property*; 2) responsibility of law enforcement falling to the victim backed by *reciprocal arrangements for protection and support in a dispute*; 3) standard *adjudicative procedures* established in order to *avoid violent forms of dispute resolution*; 4) *offenses treated as torts* [that is, as offenses against a specific person or persons and not "society"] and typically punishable by *economic payments in restitution*; 5) strong *incentives to yield to prescribed punishment* when guilty of an offense due to the reciprocally established *threat of social ostracism*; and 6) legal change arising through an *evolutionary process of developing customs and norms*. (Benson 1990, 21, emphasis in original)

These are not only the characteristics that theorists such as Rothbard and Barnett suggest are necessary components of a successful non-monopolistic legal order, but indeed actual features of the legal systems that developed in Europe and the Middle East, and also of the 'anarchic' dispute resolution mechanisms of the American West prior to the expansion of Federal power (as noted by Anderson and Hill).

The conclusion one is directed towards by the theorizing of Rothbard and Barnett and the examples cited by Anderson and Hill and Benson is that law ought to be construed as a "natural consequence of the attempts of people to live and work together," as Charles Plott phrases it, and that it is something that, although necessary for society, does not presuppose a coercive monopoly of power. It is through this strategy of argumentation that one might address the challenge presented by defenses of the state based in what I have characterized as a Hobbesian Fear. Again, though, it is interesting to note how these conceptions are not necessarily at odds with the theories of a 'morally legitimate state' found in Machan and Narveson. Machan says we tacitly consent to the morally legitimate aspects of the state because that is necessary for getting on with life. Would rational agents consent to the morally legitimate state, one which was only in the business of protecting rights and violated no one's? Perhaps they would, but we cannot assume on that basis that people in any given state tacitly consent simply because they remain where they are. People might give express consent to all sorts of regimes, but the claim that by living in an area, one gives tacit consent to the laws of the that area's government is unconvincing. In any case, Machan only claims that we may assume that people *would* tacitly consent to morally legitimate states. How can we assume tacit consent to any *existing* state? Locke's argument for this misses the point:

> For it would be a direct Contradiction, for any one, to enter into Society with others for the securing and regulating of Property: And yet to suppose his Land, whose Property is to be regulated by the Laws of the Society, should be exempt from the Jurisdiction of that Government, to which he himself the Proprietor of the Land, is a subject. (Section 120)

Locke's argument was that the whole point of joining a society was to secure better one's life, liberty, and property. Obviously, one cannot simultaneously agree to be governed and expect not be subject to the government. But what if one prefers not to join in the first place? Locke's account of tacit consent says nothing to those who explicitly withhold consent, and later appropriations of the tacit consent argument inevitably fall short in this respect. As Hume put it, "we may as well assert that a man, by remaining in a vessel, freely consents to the dominion of the master; though he was carried on board while asleep, and must leap into the ocean and perish the moment he leaves her" ("Of the Original Contract," 363). This is a useful metaphor because the covenants that Locke argues are necessary to establish actual consent were made (if ever) before anyone now alive was born.

The fundamental dispute, then, appears to be centered around what form the final arbiter for conflict resolution takes, since all agree that some such mechanism is necessary, and what sorts of social institutions will adequately provide the mechanisms for such conflict resolution, since all concerned agree that this, if not centralized political authority, is a necessary condition of society. Having seen how the challenge posed at the end of Chapter 3 might be met, I can turn now to an extended example about cooperation, and then to asking some final questions about anarchism and minimal-state theory from the perspective of the libertarian theorists involved.

5

Disaster Relief in a Free Society: An Extended Example

By way of considering a concrete example of stateless social order, we might ask: how would a regime of individual liberty handle various destructive natural phenomena, such as earthquakes, floods, or hurricanes?[19] This question seems like the sort of challenge one might make to a defender of liberty, someone who may have argued that the state is not necessary for dealing with such problems. Note that the question presupposes that the state does in fact respond to these catastrophes. When a president or governor declares some scene of major destruction a disaster area, she or he is not merely stating the obvious—the official designation of 'disaster area' makes the affected area eligible for various sorts of relief aid. There is a Federal Emergency Management Agency. Like operation of the military, the police, and the court system, coping with natural disasters has in fact been a traditional role of the government. So the defender of the sort of political theory in which the state's role is to be vastly diminished (or eliminated entirely) will typically be expected to explain how such a society would handle natural emergencies.

19. This chapter is reprinted, with minor revisions, from my essay "Liberty, Policy, and Natural Disasters," in *Liberty and Hard Cases*, edited by Tibor R. Machan, with the permission of the publisher, Hoover Institution Press. Copyright 2002 by the Board of Trustees of the Leland Stanford Junior University.

But among the other presuppositions of the question are, first, that the state does an effective enough job of responding that the burden of proof falls to the libertarian and, second, that 'handling' is a simple matter of bringing resources to bear on the problem effectively. Often, the state's performance of some limited function evolves into a massive bureaucracy devoted as much to itself as to its object. Need it be the case with disaster relief as well? By way of answering the initial question, I shall endeavor to address these other presuppositions and side issues.

A common complaint against the state is that bureaucracies devoted to a specific problem have a tendency to work for their own self-preservation. For example, many critics have argued that the bureaucracy of the welfare state designs antipoverty programs that keep a certain percentage of the people poor, so that there will always be someone to help. But regardless of whether this is a valid charge, in an important sense the analogy does not apply to disaster relief, namely, that government bureaucrats do not literally *cause* earthquakes and hurricanes. However, there *is* a sense in which government agencies do cause damage. Since there is institutionalized, government-subsidized disaster relief and flood insurance, coastal property in hurricane threat zones has become much more developed, with the result that, when hurricanes hit, there are more buildings to destroy than there would likely be if private insurance companies were entirely responsible for these properties (this conundrum will be addressed below). "The broader problem [with the seeming need for government disaster relief] is that many property owners living in disaster-prone areas would probably choose not to insure against catastrophe risks if faced with actuarially fair premiums . . . [so] many people would end up without insurance."[20] This creates, in turn, a greater demand for government involvement in disaster relief.

The circularity here is especially vicious: government disaster insurance and relief make it easier to choose to live in a risky area, but the increased number of people at risk make government dis-

---

20. Moss 1999, 344.

aster programs apparently more indispensable. If there were no special incentives to place oneself at risk, fewer people would, and there would be less disaster relief needed. So, clearly, a society that prioritized liberty would have fewer problems of that sort. Nevertheless, it is true that there would still be natural disasters even without the government and true that any society, even a maximally libertarian one, would need to have some mechanism for handling the problems that would arise as a result.

What does it mean to 'handle' these sorts of problems? For the most part, it *doesn't* mean prevention. Again, since we are talking about natural disasters, to a large extent we must simply accept the fact that they will happen. In this context, it only means dealing with the aftermath of the phenomena, which means helping people medically, helping people financially, and cleaning up the damage. Understood this way, disaster relief is a matter of concentrating resources on a particular region or specific set of victims.

This is sometimes known as a 'collective action problem', 'collective' because it often entails the coordination of resources from large numbers of people, 'problem' because there needs to be some organized way to coordinate the actions or donations so they are properly directed. How is this collective action problem different from others? One, it needs to be immediate. When a hurricane has left 150 people homeless, a five-year plan fails to address the problem. Two, it is supposed to be temporary, a discrete response to a particular event. Once the people (say) have new homes, the emergency is over.

Several liberty concerns arise as a result of all this. First of all, is society's need to respond to this sort of situation an argument in favor of the state? Can these problems be addressed without the state? Second, does the state exploit its current role in this matter to expand the scope of its authority beyond its original justification? These are the key issues that remain.

It seems odd to suggest that state action is the only way to address a problem (in this chapter, I am not bothering with the U.S.-specific distinction between state governments and the federal government; I am using "state" in the generic political sense). But we grow accustomed to certain matters being the purview of the state, and then it becomes difficult to conceptualize the state not being involved. But our challenged imaginations are not the same thing as an argument.

For example, the government has long been the operator of the postal service, and it is difficult for many people to imagine how they would get mail if there were no post office. But in the past two decades, the vast growth of UPS and Federal Express shows that it is possible for a private company to establish a nationwide system for routing, distribution, and speedy delivery of packages.

The conceptual failing is actually largely semantic: people cannot imagine life without the United States Postal Service (or could not imagine this thirty years ago), but what they are really having trouble conceiving is life without mail. But there's a difference between privatizing the postal system and eliminating the postal system, and no one actually suggests the latter. Similarly, with phone service: anyone over the age of thirty will remember the expression 'the phone company'. Now a remark involving that phrase would be criticized for vagueness since there are many competing phone companies.

Because there is a demand for telephone service and mail delivery, we can imagine that a free market would provide them, although there will be some argument about whether there should be a regulated or unrestricted market in those services. But what about disaster relief? Would disaster relief also emerge in a free society, or is this an example of 'market failure' requiring the intervention of the state? Some argue that there is a moral obligation to aid the needy. If that is so, then government disaster relief would be justified on the grounds that we are all fulfilling our moral obligations when we pay our taxes to support such programs. However, saying that something is justified is not to say that something is necessary.

In other words, the government relief program may be permissible (one way to fulfill our moral duties), but it may not be obligatory (the only way to fulfill our moral duties). So the question need not devolve to one of moral duties. The question would remain how best to discharge those duties. To argue that state action is the only way to meet these duties is to argue that social cooperation requires state intervention.

This is essentially what Hobbes was claiming when he argued for the necessity of an absolute sovereign. Without a centralized authority to "keep us in awe," the argument goes, we would not be able to cooperate on even as simple a task as maintaining the peace. Since it is paradigmatically in our own best interests not to have all others trying to kill us, a version of Hobbes's argument tends to be invoked whenever the issue of social cooperation arises. If we can't even cooperate at the minimal level needed to secure peace, why should we be able to cooperate on more complex tasks such as educating the young or feeding the poor or building roads or responding to natural disasters?

As I have been endeavoring to show, the problem with this line of reasoning is that the initial premise is mistaken. As we've seen, ample research demonstrates that cooperation can arise independently of state intervention. For instance, as discussed in Chapter 4, Axelrod's computer simulation showed conclusively that cooperation was the strategy that produced the best outcomes over the long term. It was actually a certain kind of cooperation that was most robust, a responsive approach to cooperation that tries to encourage others to cooperate but is capable of punishing them if they refuse. We also saw how subsequent research (such as Nowak and Sigmund) confirmed that, even assuming the most self-interested motivations, cooperation can develop naturally. So since the argument that government intervention is necessary to ensure that people will cooperate fails in general, it cannot be invoked as a rationale for the necessity of the state for the coordination of disaster relief efforts.

So how are the relief efforts to be coordinated in a free society?

In times past, charity was typically handled through private means: religious groups, mutual aid societies, and philanthropic millionaires.[21] In the newsletter of the Capital Research Center, Daniel Oliver has documented how, for example, the city of

---

21. For more on mutual aid societies, see the essential Beito 2000.

Chicago was rebuilt after the 1871 fire almost entirely through nongovernmental charitable initiatives.[22] Plainly, it is at least possible that disasters could be dealt with independently of the government. So it would seem as though the state is not necessary, at least in the strict sense: if any disaster has been responded to effectively by private means, then it is false that the state is necessary for disaster relief.

Nevertheless, one would hope for a more interesting answer: in today's world, is it necessary that the government operate disaster relief activities as it does? Again, the status quo influences one's reactions to such a question. Since the state in fact does assume the service of disaster relief, we come to think of that as a fundamental task of the government, perhaps even a defining one. Even people who might be sympathetic to the claim that the government should be limited will regard certain functions of the state as essential—for example, operating an army.

Disaster relief may well have taken on that appearance. Indeed, in the modern world, the more visible the state's role in disaster relief, the more likely people will be to see it as a fundamental: when we turn on TV news reports about how a catastrophe is being handled, we are most likely to remember the well-organized efforts of a National Guard unit that had been mobilized to respond. Of course, we also see pictures of private citizens pitching in to help their community voluntarily, but these are often judged less camera-worthy.

But here is another circularity: one motivation for joining the National Guard is so that you will be able to help out your community in case of emergency. So the presence of a state-run disaster relief machinery absorbs much of whatever volunteerism there is regarding such activities. Then it becomes difficult to conceptualize people having the means to help if it weren't for the state. Michael Taylor explains that "the more the state intervenes . . . , the more 'necessary' (on this view) it becomes, because positive altruism and voluntary cooperative behavior

---

22. Oliver 1999.

atrophy in the presence of the state and *grow* in its absence. Thus, again, the state exacerbates the conditions which are supposed to make it necessary."[23]

Because the state takes upon itself various duties, Taylor argues, individuals not only lose opportunities to cooperate for various ends, they lose the interest. "[The citizen] may come to feel that his responsibility to society has been discharged as soon as he has

paid his taxes (which are taken coercively from him by the state). . . . The state releases the individual from the responsibility or need to cooperate with others directly" (169).

So the question is not so much whether the private sector can do things the state cannot but whether the state's presence has a negative effect on individual incentive to help others.

Another incentive for joining the National Guard is that it pays. These same people, presumably, could be enticed to work in a similar capacity by a private disaster relief agency. But that merely pushes the question back one level. The state agencies get their funding through taxes, which is to say they get funding without regard to demand for their services or ability to deliver results. A private agency would have to either be staffed by volunteers or get its money from people willing to pay, who would have to either be philanthropists or people paying for something they valued. Would people be interested in responding, through labor or money, to an emergency?

It seems reasonable to suspect that people would be willing to respond to emergencies that affect them—for instance, cleaning up their town after it has been flooded. But people may have less of an interest in helping communities more remote from their experience or may be willing to help but literally unable if, for instance, the damage is more severe than the people have the resources to deal with. These seem like the underlying concerns that might be taken to justify the state's involvement: the former is a variation on the traditional 'market-failure' argument for state intervention, and the latter is a straightforward allocation-of-resources situation.

---

23. Taylor 1987, 168.

Is there good reason to think that there is sufficiently little social cooperation, even regarding helping out in an emergency, as to amount to 'market failure'? By 'market failure' in the context of social cooperation, especially in emergency situations, we must be referring to something like 'an insufficient amount of people willing to devote resources to help respond to emergencies.' For example, it is often said that 'nonexcludable' public goods such as lighthouses would not get built in a free market because the threat of free-riders would be a substantial disincentive to the providers. (Of course, lighthouses *were* built by the private sector, but the persistence of this argument is as strong as a cold virus.) Therefore, government action is needed to ensure that the goods are provided despite the market failure. If the good is needed, but not enough people are willing to pay for it, it will not appear. So since there is a general need, the government provides the good using tax money.

Disaster relief might be thought of in these terms: everyone would like to see the hurricane-ravaged town rebuilt, but no one seems willing to put up enough money to fund it, so the government has to step in.

Is it true that, left to their own devices, people would not be willing to help each other when there has been a flood or hurricane in their community? This seems implausible. But it is possible that a community may be so devastated that it is incapable of helping itself and requires assistance from outside the community. Would anyone from outside the affected community be willing to help? That would be an empirical matter: clearly some people would be and others less so.

It is hard to forecast the percentages because, first, every emergency is different and, second, some of the willingness to help has been siphoned off by things like the National Guard having already attracted a large portion of those who would be willing to help and taxes having been collected to pay for federal disaster relief programs. This is a considerable factor in gauging people's willingness to help. If I am forced to pay to contribute to government disaster relief efforts, I may feel that I've already 'done my part' when the call goes out for help. If the government is inefficient about allocating the taxed resources, and cannot afford to respond adequately, then there will be a need for more help; but many people will refuse ('I gave at the office'), and this would be a second sense in which the government's attempts to coordinate disaster relief end up making things worse.

It also depends on how 'community' is conceived. The more localized the community is, the more likely people are to feel an imperative to lend a hand. If one's own town, or even the next town over ('my neighbors'), is flooded or blown away by a hurricane, it is not easy to imagine people refusing to help, especially because in one sense, altruism and self-interest nearly coincide. Each person in the town has a clear interest in rebuilding the town, an interest that cannot be neatly categorized as self-interest or altruism. It may be Jim's Coffee Shop, but I eat there every day. The more remote the disaster, the less likely this sentiment seems to be: someone in Idaho may not feel as compelled to help rebuild a hurricane-ravaged town in Florida, since that isn't in any recognizable sense part of the same community. It is, of course, part of the nation, but to some extent that is an artificial distinction.

To people in, say, northern Idaho, neighboring Canadians may be felt to be more a part of the community than the more remote, albeit politically related, Floridians are. Some Idahoans may, of course, want to help the Floridians out of pure sympathy. Some may be motivated by a self-interest; for instance, a lumber mill owner may see an opportunity for bulk sales and offer cheap prices.

There are also more complex mixes of altruism and self-interest. In a recent television commercial, Miller Beer reminds us of the time when some southern town was flooded, and Miller sent in truckloads of drinking water, bottled in beer bottles after it had retooled the brewery. This cannot be interpreted categorically as altruism, since Miller derives valuable public relations and good will from the act and the continued retelling of the act on TV (message: we care). But neither can it be interpreted as narrowly self-interested as there are cheaper ways to advertise, and it's entirely plausible that some Miller executives genuinely felt they should help in this way. Examples like this one demonstrate that the categories of altruism and self-interest do not always do the work they are supposed to.

It's not a clean dichotomy between looking to help others and serving my own interests exclusively. One can have a self-interest in helping another, or one can simultaneously benefit oneself and another, or one can have feelings of sympathy that do not contradict self-regard. In fact, people seem to manifest these different traits precisely in emergency situations: we all have to pitch in to save the town. Is that helping the community or helping myself? Again, if I perceive it as my town, my community, then I can easily be motivated to help. But this brings us back to the question of the definition of community in a twofold way.

First, what is the scope, and, second, who decides? As to the first dimension, the scope of the community, for most people there seems to be a vaguely defined threshold. The nearer the disaster to the person's experience, the more keenly is felt the need to help. The more remote the disaster, the more likely the person will regard it as someone else's problem, however calamitous. Most of us would gladly offer shelter to our next-door neighbors if their house burned down, but when we hear about an earthquake in Turkey, we typically do not offer to fly people over to stay with us. (The defeater to the geographic threshold condition is, of course, family ties: we would be more likely to want to help a family member or any close friend regardless of distance.)

One argument for government disaster relief would be that it ties together communities that are geographically remote under a common bond, thus enabling people in Idaho to feel more connected to Floridians and facilitating transfers of assistance.

But why should political distinctions be a paramount consideration? If the argument is that one has a moral obligation to help the needy, surely a needy person in Guatemala has as much a claim to that help as a person in Florida. But if the argument is not one of universal moral obligation but of political alliance, then the Floridian has a more tangible claim on our help than the Guatemalan. And this would seem to give rise to the argument for the state's involvement: since we are in a political union, we will all contribute x dollars to a pool of common money for disaster relief, and any community in our union may draw on that fund should there be an emergency. That sounds prudent.

Why, though, should we think that only the state may operate such a fund? When the state operates the fund, it ceases to be voluntary, and hence the liberty objection: why should I be *forced* to contribute? The nonvoluntary nature of the present arrangement is partly why political means are inefficient. A purely voluntary system of mutual aid would be unlikely to offer cheap assistance to developers of beach property in hurricane zones. If the argument for the state's involvement in disaster relief is that it is an efficient way to coordinate social action, it couldn't be more mistaken.

Another sort of argument for the state's involvement, or perhaps a tacit component of the previous, is that the state's coercive means are necessary because otherwise there just won't be enough assistance to go around. We turn to that argument next.

If we look at disaster relief as a matter of distribution of social resources, we can say either that a free market will address the problem or that it won't, and hence government action is necessary. The former response would require an argument like this: since people want their houses rebuilt or their towns cleaned up, there is a market for the provision of these services, and, hence, absent state interference in the market, they would be provided at a price people chose to pay in accordance with the value they place on them.

But, sound or not, that argument will fail to persuade the very people who find it difficult to conceptualize nongovernmental disaster relief, so perhaps it would be most profitable to examine the facets of the latter response. Say the free market wouldn't adequately allocate resources to respond to the financial hardships of disaster relief. Even given a role for the state in this area, we have two distinct models for government involvement; call them the school paradigm and the food paradigm. On the school paradigm, the reasoning is that, since society has a duty to provide a decent education for all, the state must operate schools. There are three possible objections to this.

First, one could argue that there is no social duty to provide education for others, no obligation for Smith to support the education of Jones's children. Second, one could observe that the inference is logically fallacious, absent a premise equating social action with state action. These objections will go unexamined for the present discussion. But a third objection one might make is that even accepting that there is a social obligation to provide education, it is not clear that operating schools is the best way to do this. One alternative possibility would be on what I have called the food paradigm. If there is anything more essential to life than education, it would surely be food, and anyone who agrees that there is a social obligation to make sure everyone is educated is likely to agree also that everyone should be fed. Yet the model for state action here is wholly different.

No one today seriously argues that the state should run farms and operate supermarkets. Countries that do still operate this way are plagued by shortages, whereas our current system produces an overabundance. It is commonly acknowledged that our current system is the most efficient way to produce and distribute food, although some people are so poor that they cannot afford sufficient food. But the mechanism for social assistance for such people is to enable them to afford it through direct cash payments or food stamps.

One advantage of the food paradigm over the school paradigm is that the former recognizes the superior efficiency of the free market in production and distribution, while responding to social concerns about poverty, whereas the latter responds to those concerns in a way which, in an effort to avoid the social costs of the market, eliminates the benefits as well. Even given statist presuppositions, the food paradigm is clearly the more efficient model of the two. Which should be the operative model for disaster relief should be evident. If the argument for government involvement in disaster relief is a concern that people simply cannot afford to help themselves, then the solution is direct cash payments, rather than an institutionalized bureaucracy, which, as we have seen, indirectly exacerbates the very problems it is intended to address.

If there were no government disaster relief, what would be the alternatives? Certainly there would be private charitable agencies, such as the Red Cross or the United Way. If people weren't currently taxed to pay for disaster relief, they would have to assume personal responsibility for contributing, and the result would be variable: one imagines that some would contribute more than they pay under the current system but that others would contribute less.

Given other reductions of the scope of government, we might see more entrepreneurial mixtures of altruism and self-interest, such as a foreign corporation seeking to establish goodwill might follow the lead of Miller Beer, providing or underwriting assistance in return for the public relations benefit. Ultimately it is impossible to predict exactly what sorts of institutions might arise to respond to such emergencies. There may be a role for emergency cash transfer payments but not for an institutionalized government presence. The argument that disasters could not possibly be addressed without the state's intervention is false since historical examples to the contrary abound, and the argument that the state is the most efficient way to coordinate resources is flawed for the reasons I have tried to elaborate here.

What if the worst is true? What if a free society turned out to be incapable of responding adequately to these disasters? It seems reasonable to want an answer to this question. But first, let's think about what such a question means.

Again, it partly depends on how we define 'adequate response'. That seems to mean 'efficiently and effectively coordinate the provision of relief services'. We have seen that there is no reason to think that a nongovernmental organization could not do this, and some reason to think that government involvement makes things worse. But, for the sake of argument, if this analysis were wrong, what would that imply about the scope of government authority? Less than the statist might think.

It might justify the existence of a government mechanism for coordination of relief efforts without justifying the provision of those efforts. It might justify the provision of relief only in those cases where the private efforts are inadequate. It might justify temporary, ad hoc, deployment of resources without justifying a large institutionalized structure. This last observation speaks to the responsibility issue, which needs revisiting. Of all the problems one can point to in a bureaucratized disaster relief system, the most dangerous, and the most clearly identifiable as unjustified, is the way in which state-sponsored disaster insurance creates an incentive to develop property in known potential disaster areas like hurricane zones and floodplains. The erosion of personal responsibility this engenders is the reductio ad absurdum of this pattern.

Conservative and libertarian critics of the welfare state have long argued that the fact that the state makes it more attractive to not work than to work at a low-wage job creates a sense that people are not responsible for their own upkeep (Charles Murray, to take one example).[24] The state will look after them. Whether this is apt or not, it is plain that federally subsidized flood insurance and the like give people an incentive to build and develop in places they otherwise would not. Oceanfront lots, for example, are very attractive to people who like the ocean. But one generally wants to insure such an investment.

Insurance companies base their premiums on the information they can gather about similar things, "similar" because although each case is different, one can extrapolate statistically from trends and probabilities. For example, health insurance premiums may be more expensive for a smoker, not because the insurance company knows that *this person* will incur greater medical expenses but because smokers tend to. Auto insurance premiums are higher if you own a late-model car and live in New York City, not because they know that *your car* will be stolen but because there is a demonstrable rate of thefts of certain models.

So in these two cases, statistically, it is more of a risk to insure you even though each individual case is unpredictable, and the insurance companies reflect that enhanced risk in their rate structure. You can get insurance despite the risk; it is simply going to cost more. Now a geographic area may also have demonstrable patterns—for example, the chance of your home being damaged by an earthquake is greater if you live in San Francisco, or New Madrid, Missouri, than if you live in Manhattan, although the burglary rate may be higher in Manhattan. So in Manhattan you would expect to pay more for theft insurance but less for earth-

----

24. Murray 1984.

quake insurance. (No one is currently proposing that there be federally subsidized theft insurance for city dwellers.)

Similarly, your hurricane insurance will likely be less than if you lived in South Florida or along the Carolina coast. In a purely free society, of course, people would be free to live on the Carolina coast or in New Madrid, but it would be up to them to bear the cost of the higher insurance premiums. Currently, a variety of government programs make it more attractive to assume these risks than they otherwise would be. Federal flood insurance, for example, is available to those people who live in communities that participate in the National Flood Insurance Program. Although payouts do not come directly from tax dollars, the rates are lower because of the pooled risk of the participating communities.[25] (This sort of pooled risk could be coordinated by any large insurance concern, so the question is whether the government runs it because it is so unprofitable that no insurance company wants to or whether the government runs it because it is assumed to be the only organization capable of doing so.)

To the extent that the cost of bearing an increased risk is artificially reduced, people will come to see greater incentive in assuming that risk. People are actually encouraged to incur greater risks and then are eligible for assistance when the worst comes to pass. When you suffer automobile damage, your car insurance rates rise, on the theory that this is evidence that your risk is somewhat higher than the norm. But if one is a flood victim, one may continue to reside in the risky area at a cost that does not reflect this because of the cost-pooling arrangements of the NFIP.

Communitarians would likely endorse the notion that, since we are all part of the community, we all have an obligation to help people afford housing and help victims of natural disasters. One slogan of the communitarian movement, though, is "rights *and* responsibilities."[26] Naturally one has the right to live in a flood

---

25. For a fuller discussion of the National Flood Insurance Program and its social cost, see Arnold 2002.

26. See, for example, the journal *The Responsive Community*. Communitarianism will be discussed more in the next chapter.

hazard area or a hurricane zone, but one should also have the responsibility to bear the increased risks involved. The government's subsidizing the assumption of higher risk entails an erosion of personal responsibility, which then feeds into the notion that the government is necessary to help people. The impression is that the government is needed to help people who are in trouble as a result of its own policies.

What can we conclude? It seems as though the government is not *necessary* for the provision of disaster relief, that there is every reason to think that a libertarian-oriented society would be capable of responding to natural disasters, that extant government disaster programs exacerbate many of the problems they are meant to alleviate, and that these programs have a tendency to erode personal responsibility. They erode responsibility both in those who are encouraged to assume risks they otherwise would not and, ironically, in those who help others less than they otherwise would because they have come to think that the government will take care of it.

Like so many government programs, the government disaster apparatus entails dramatic countervailing effects that undermine its legitimacy yet is firmly entrenched both in terms of the public perception and in terms of the self-preservation instincts of all bureaucracies. What can be done? It would seem politically unfeasible to simply abolish FEMA and its many programs.

Some short-term suggestions, some of which I have alluded to, thus seem appropriate. Other than switching from a schools paradigm to a food paradigm, which is politically no more feasible than abolition, one more interesting, and I think more productive, suggestion would be to alter the mission of FEMA to be one of coordinating, rather than providing, relief. (Perhaps other brewers will compete for the privilege of providing bottled water to stricken towns.) This would allow the bureaucracy to continue to exist but would restore the concept of private provision of emergency assistance to one of voluntary helping with a true sense of community. This would restore some sense of the importance of voluntary assistance in a free society, which communitarians as well as libertarians ought to endorse.

Another short-term modification would be to limit the role of the state in these matters to the truly unexpected. We can know with reasonable certainty that certain regions are likely to be stricken with floods or hurricanes or earthquakes, whereas in other areas it may be completely unexpected, the result of an incredibly unlikely confluence of events or conditions. We could limit the FEMA mission to one of responding to the unpredictable emergencies, rather than the ones that could have been expected. This way, government assistance would be available when the inconceivable happens, but people who want to live in a floodplain or a hurricane zone or on a fault line would be forced to assume their fair share of the risks that that entails. This would address the personal responsibility issue from the other side, while reducing the scope of government involvement.

Both these short-term suggestions would still leave the state apparatus in place, which is not ideal. But these changes might, after a time, bring about a change in public perception and attitude. There might then come a time when the countervailing effects of government-run disaster relief would be more readily apparent, and there could be sufficient support for privatization. As with other government programs, part of the continued support for federal disaster relief stems from a lack of public awareness of alternatives and of the history of the program. People seem to support programs more firmly when they cannot see how else a problem would be addressed. The two interim proposals I suggest would provide at least a glimpse of an alternative, opening the door to further discussion about the role of the state and its putative necessity. In the next chapter, we can return to the concept of a legal system and its relation to political authority. I will also at that point be able to address communitarian criticisms.

6

Incommensurability and the Problem of the Practical

A Conceptual Difficulty in Application

One thing that seems puzzling about the way the historical findings presented by Anderson and Hill, Benson, Beito, and the others are intended to support the theoretical framework of Barnett and Rothbard is the fact that although these societies had the makings of an 'anarchic' legal system, they ended up states. In other words, if polycentric, non-coercive conflict resolution mechanisms work so well, why do they end up being consolidated by political authority? Is it because they are unstable, or is it perhaps for some other reason?

Nozick's idea that the competing protective agencies would, as a matter of market efficiency, eventually be consolidated into one dominant protective agency is not the applicable explanation for this phenomenon. Nozick's model presupposes a modern, capitalist economy which includes a free market in protection and adjudication services. The fact that there were competing avenues for finding justice in England prior to the consolidation of law by the crown does not amount to the same thing. Nozick is speculating about future market arrangements, not explaining the development of law in Europe, which though non-monopolistic, had several features that distinguishes it from what theorists like Barnett have in mind. It is possible that stateless societies are inherently prone to coercive political consolidation, but it is also possible that kings were able to assume control over all functions of enforcement and adjudication because the pervasive ideology of the times gave them a mantle of legitimacy in doing so. In an era where information and education were in short supply, and a widespread ideology of hereditary aristocracy (and the fear of God) gave kings an additional veneer of legitimacy, the expansion of royal power might be easier then it would be after the enlightenment. Maybe a stronger (liberal) ideology would resist such monarchist attempts at consolidation. David Friedman suggests that it was not the invasion of a stronger alien power that destroyed the decentralized legal system of Iceland, but an alien ideology, namely, monarchism (Friedman 1989, 207).

But how exactly could this happen? If the decentralized legal systems worked, what would be the appeal of a centralized one? If liberalism would eventually supersede monarchism during the Enlightenment, why would centralized political authority develop the kind of stability it did? Let us consider briefly the consolidation by the Crown of competing courts in England. In the Middle Ages, Englishmen could seek justice in baronial courts, ecclesiastical courts, or merchant courts, in addition to the royal courts. As Harold Berman explains in his 1983 book, *Law and Revolution,*

> Legal pluralism originated in the differentiation of the ecclesiastical polity from the secular polities. The church declared its freedom from secular control, its exclusive jurisdiction in some matters, and its concurrent jurisdiction in other matters. . . . Secular law itself was divided up into various competing types, including royal law, feudal law, manorial law, urban law, and mercantile law. (Berman 1983, 10)

According to Berman, this pluralism

> was a source of freedom. A serf might run to the town court for protection against his master. A vassal might run to the king's court for protection against his lord. A cleric might run to the ecclesiastical court for protection against the king. (Berman 1983, 10)

The pluralism offered some measure of freedom by virtue of making power more diffuse. (The 'separation of powers' in the American system has a similar effect.) What might account for the gradual consolidation of power by the crown?

Arthur R. Hogue, in his 1966 book *Origins of the Common Law*, tells us that

> Litigants were not compelled to seek the king's justice; only in matters touching freehold did the Crown enjoy a monopoly over judicial business. But because English subjects gave them business, gradually the medieval royal courts starved out, rather than crushed out, their competitors. Thus by the end of the thirteenth century the royal courts were rapidly becoming courts of first instance for free men of the realm. (Hogue 1966, 18–19)

It is tempting to see this as an example in actual history of Nozick's theory of the Dominant Protective Agency, but there is more to it. This consolidation of the means of conflict resolution took place in the context of the development of the common law, which has certain features that enhance its appeal. While it was codified and institutionalized by the royal courts, the common law emerges from principles and practices of (already) widespread appeal. According to Hogue, the common law best serves the needs of a dynamic society because it is both stable and vital, that is, it contains elements that carry on across time, enabling people to have reasonable expectations about the future, and also elements that enable the procedures and policies to adapt to changing times.

> The doctrine of *stare decisis*, or the practice of looking to precedents while formulating a legal procedure . . . assumes that court decisions have been reasonable, that what was reasonable in one century may be reasonable in another—even though in the meantime the most revolutionary social and political changes may have occurred. (Hogue 1966, 9)

> The other desirable objective . . . is adaptability of the law to meet new social conditions. (Hogue 1966, 10)

This combination, Hogue argues, paved the way for innovations that were desirable to the lawyers and to the people at large. Developments such as trial by jury and the writ system, by which authorities were obliged to show just cause prior to acting, offered the English both security and efficiency in their pursuits of justice. This helps to explain why people came to prefer the royal courts to the others.

> They provided the best justice available, for several reasons. First, the medieval jury, a body of neighbors sworn to give evidence under oath, was preferable to older modes of trial such as ordeal, combat, or compurgation [proving innocence by having a number of people swear to a belief in it]. Second, the professional skill of royal judges was superior to that of feudal lords and manorial bailiffs. . . . Third, the incontestable validity of royal records was preferable to the . . . fallible memories of suitors of local courts. (Hogue 1966, 19)

Hogue also points out that the enforcement was carried out by an authority of great wealth and power, giving people good reason to believe that the enforcement would actually take place. But none of these features are dependent for their existence on monarchy. The royal courts triumphed because they were the ones using principles and procedures that people wanted used. But royal courts could then claim that like the feudal system itself, royal monopoly of justice was 'natural'. It seems, then, that Hogue and Friedman are both partially correct about the means by which decentralized authority becomes centralized. Clearly, the crown had more in its favor than simply a court system which gave good justice. It also had the concept of monarchism—that the king had a natural claim to all the land, and that the property rights of any others originated in royal gift or lease. Given this, any assault by Smith on Jones would not simply be an attack on Jones, a violation of Jones's property in his person, but also an attack on the king, a 'breaking of the king's peace'. In this manner, the sovereign can be seen not only as divine inheritor and steward of all the land, but also as having a special, privileged status regarding the functions of adjudication and law enforcement. The royal courts could thus expand their jurisdiction in a way that no other court could.

Even today, every expansion of state power, even when resisted in some quarters, has at its base a widely accepted (and generally unexamined) claim that it is both necessary and proper. All political entities try to increase their own legitimacy with this claim. Today arguments about market failure and 'tacit consent' have taken the place of theories of the divine right of kings. But even if it turned out that centralized political authority was an inevitable historical development, that would not serve as a justification in the sense of being morally or rationally acceptable to those subject to it.

Is the state inevitable? I would argue that it is a historical contingency that states developed the way they did. But the more important question is whether they can be justified given our current understanding. If it turns out that the answer is that they cannot, then all that remains is to erode the conceptual legitimacy that the state has acquired. This conceptual legitimacy is what Barnett refers to as the "halo effect," wherein the government's use of power "will be perceived by most to be at least presumptively justified" (Barnett 1985, 54). Rothbard makes a similar observation: "it must be emphasized that a crucial element in the power of the state is its legitimacy in the eyes of the majority of the public, the fact that after centuries of propaganda, the depredations of the state are looked upon as rather benevolent services" (Rothbard 1978, 205).

However, recall Michael Taylor's explanation for the seeming inevitability of the state, briefly noted in the previous chapter, that

> the more the state intervenes . . ., the more "necessary" (on this view) it becomes, because positive altruism and voluntary cooperative behavior *atrophy* in the presence of the state and *grow* in its absence. Thus, again, the state exacerbates the conditions which are supposed to make it necessary. (Taylor 1987, 168)

Because the state takes upon itself various duties, Taylor argues, individuals not only lose opportunities to cooperate for various ends, they lose the interest. "[The citizen] may come to feel that his responsibility to society has been discharged as soon as he has paid his taxes (which are taken coercively from him by the state). . . . The state releases the individual from the responsibility or need to cooperate with others directly . . ." (Taylor 1987, 169).

Many contemporary anarchist theorists eschew this line of argument for fear of being seen as proposing that a new breed of human would develop once freed from the corrupting shackles of the state. For example, Rothbard says he wants to "defuse" a common criticism,

> the common charge that anarchists "assume all people are good" and that without the state no crime would be committed. In short, that anarchism assumes that with the abolition of the state a New Anarchist Man will emerge, cooperative, humane, and benevolent, so that no problem of crime will then plague the society. . . . In my view, the anarchist society is one which maximizes the tendencies for the good and the cooperative, while it minimizes both the opportunity and the moral legitimacy of the evil and the criminal. (Rothbard 1978, 193)

Rothbard goes on to say that the charge is without merit. He emphasizes the economics of the situation in order to avoid making extravagant claims about human goodness. Taylor, of course, is also not assuming that 'all people are good', but simply suggesting that living under different social structures can promote different attitudes and behavior, which is, I think, quite reasonable. So "government is an evil which is necessary only as long as people behave in the way in which they have come to behave as a result of living for a long time under government" (Taylor 1987, 173).

Don Lavoie has argued that a conception of a shared political culture is necessary for the development of a workable political theory.

> What makes a legal system, *any* legal system, work is a shared system of belief in the rules of justice - a political culture. The culture is, in turn, an evolving process, a tradition which is continually being reappropriated in creative ways in the interpersonal and public discourses through which social individuals communicate. Anarchism seems workable to its advocates only because they implicitly assume a certain democratic political culture will prevail. (Lavoie 1993, 116)

But of course all political theories assume a certain prevailing culture. For example, Nozick's predictions about the Dominant

Protective Agency presuppose a free-market society in which the services of conflict resolution are traded like other services. Rothbard's assumptions about the prevailing political culture are in his view very minimal, and more to the point, the same ones that Nozick is committed to. But Lavoie's larger point, that theories only seem workable under certain sets of assumptions, is a good one. It took Benson's empirical research to persuade Lavoie that under certain cultural conditions, the anarchist legal theory would represent a feasible project, and he argues that anarchist theory remains unpersuasive to most people "not primarily because of any shortcomings of the arguments its proponents make, but because of shortcomings of our background notions of markets and democracy" (Lavoie 1993, 115). It is unclear whether cultural conditions are sufficient to satisfy Lavoie's concerns, although he argues that it is definitely possible that they could become so.

The Problem of Incommensurability

States have been justified by many theories over time, with the different theoretical justifications providing a variety of constraints on the scope of state power over the individual. To dispute any given theory of the scope of the state, one needs to show that the theoretical justification offered is either mistaken or misapplied. An example of the first of these is Locke responding to Filmer. Royal absolutism can be refuted if the king can be shown not to rule by divine right. An example of the second is Nozick responding to Rawls. An expanded conception of the welfare state based on the priority of liberty can be shown to be inconsistent with liberty. The anarchist has the burdensome task of responding to all theories of the state, however, and this raises the possibility of incommensurability. By incommensurability I mean the impossibility of productive dialogue on an issue, not simply disagreement, typically because the fundamental assumptions of the two parties are so foreign to each other. For example, different Catholic monastic orders disagree about specific issues (such as whether the poverty of Christ implies the poverty of the church) while agreeing on all fundamental starting points (such as the existence of God, or the supremacy of Rome). There can *theoretically* be a productive outcome to discussions. By contrast, a discussion between a Franciscan Catholic and a Theravada Buddhist might get stalled on the basics, for example the nature of divinity. More to the point, the finer points of, say, Machan's criticism of Rothbard, while interesting and important to libertarians, would seem like so much scholastic irrelevance to a Marxist, to whose mind both Rothbard and Machan are bourgeois liberals who are completely mistaken about the justification of authority. Anarchists such as Barnett and Rothbard would undoubtedly prefer life in Nozick's minimal-state world to life in Michael Luntley's socialist world or even in Thomas Spragens's welfarist-liberal world, but even if such a compromise were desirable, it is not clear that it would be possible, for Luntley will not concede to a vision Spragens would endorse, and Spragens will not concede to a vision such as Nozick's.

I am not sure, however, that this implies incommensurability. There may be sufficient common understanding to extend questions of justification across a further spectrum of beliefs. If there is not, the fundamental premises that separate different theorists will be made more apparent. To illustrate, let us look at an example of how welfarist liberalism responds to libertarianism, and see whether incommensurability is revealed. In his two-part article in *The Responsive Community* (Winter 1992 and Spring 1992), Thomas A. Spragens, Jr., offers a harsh critique of libertarianism. We will need to sort out some fallacious arguments, but what is left will exhibit the fundamental premises that separate the two. Whether these premises are incommensurable remains to be seen.

Spragens maintains that libertarianism 1) "narrows and distorts liberal theory"; 2) is "inadequate as a basis for a good democratic society"; and 3) can be "destructive of democratic institutions" (Spragens 1992a, 29). Unlike some critics of libertarianism, Spragens recognizes that individual freedom is a good thing. But he sees freedom as the sort of good thing that, like chocolate cake, one can have too much of. This is partly because he misconstrues the libertarian case for freedom.[27] On close analysis, the misconstrual turns out to depend on straw-man versions of libertarian argument. I think that if we expose this, we will also see that this is not a case of radical incommensurability.

Spragens begins by charging that libertarians "decontextualize freedom" (Spragens 1992a, 30), that is to say, they isolate and elevate freedom above other values. This may seem like an uncontroversial way to characterize libertarianism, but it is inaccurate. It would be more correct to say something like: libertarians elevate freedom over other *political* values. Omissions such as this are what enable Spragens to develop the straw-man libertarian that he wants to knock down. This straw libertarian is licentious, greedy, and egocentric.

More importantly, Spragens charges that libertarians neglect the value of community. This is an important feature of the straw man, a typical criticism with no basis in libertarian theory. Libertarians do not neglect the value of community, but they do stress the disvalue of coercion. For example, consider Hayek on this point: "Most of the advantages of social life . . . rest on the fact that the individual benefits from more knowledge than he is aware of" (Hayek 1960, 22). Indeed, for Hayek, this is part of why coercion is objectionable as a political means. "Coercion thus is bad because it prevents a person from using his mental powers to the full and consequently from making the greatest contribution that he is capable to the community" (Hayek 1960, 134). All the libertarians discussed in this book know it is important to work together to achieve many goals, and that fellow-feeling makes social life more pleasant. But they question the value of forcing people to serve others' ends. Libertarians deny that it is moral to make an individual subordinate to another's control, and this becomes "libertarians neglect the value of community."

Coleman contends that there is no incommensurability entailed by this critique of libertarianism. He offers an argument why even communitarians should endorse a market economy:

---

27. A fuller version of my analysis of Spragens's arguments can be found in Skoble 1992.

Although there is something attractive about consensus or agreement, the communitarian rejects the idea that society's basic institutions are simply rational contracts. Indeed, one could say that it is the liberal preoccupation with markets that so enrages the communitarian. . . . [However,] all social institutions are schemes of cooperation, in that they are expressions of the ways in which we organize our relationships with one another over various domains of activity. In order to endure, these institutions must rely on an underlying genuine consensus. . . . In markets, individuals act on their own conception of the good within a framework of normative constraints [such as the absence of force] . . . [Markets] maximize beneficial interaction while minimizing the stress on the underlying consensus. (Coleman 1988, 657–58)

Since, on this view, markets produce social stability as well as mutual exchange, even communitarians would do well to endorse certain aspects of liberalism. The prospect of incommensurability is diminished here because Coleman is not only denying the charge that liberals neglect the value of community, but claiming that those concerned with community are neglecting a social institution that serves their professed ends.[28]

Spragens's second argument against libertarianism is that it involves "oversimplifying freedom," that is to say, the libertarian conception of liberty "becomes indistinguishable from mere license or capriciousness" (Spragens 1992a, 32). Agreeing with the libertarians, Spragens eschews the notion of "positive freedom," which he understands is typically brought out to defend "paternalistic and tyrannical impositions" (Spragens 1992a, 32). He says that on this matter, he will agree with libertarians that liberty "always refers in some essential sense to freedom *from* outside interference and not to a so-called freedom *to* attain some specified end" (Spragens 1992a, 32). This is a sensible concession, but he goes on to charge that libertarians think that liberty is "freedom to

---

28. I have argued elsewhere (Skoble 1991) that other conceptions of liberalism which stress the value of community or an ethic of self-transformation (for example the critical legal studies movement) would find their own goals better served by embracing either Rawlsian liberalism or libertarianism.

do whatever one pleases." Of course, none of the libertarians I have discussed here thinks this. Spragens does not cite a single libertarian on this matter; he simply asserts that libertarians say this. On the contrary, libertarians are quick to delineate the proper scope of human freedom. Consider for example Rothbard's "central axiom": "no man or group of men may aggress against the person or property of anyone else" (Rothbard 1973, 23). The authors we have been examining typically argue that liberty is freedom to do as you please *as long as your conduct does not harm others.* Some argue that although the state can only interfere when your conduct harms others, there are other moral constraints on action that come into play. But *none* argues for the licentious version of liberty as charged.

Spragens does, however, cite two authors who do conceive of liberty as license: Hobbes and Filmer. But as Hobbes and Filmer were both advocates of absolute monarchy, this is an inappropriate place to turn for textual support. Naturally Hobbes and Filmer characterize liberty in this way—it helps them argue in favor of not having liberty as a political value. So Spragens has established that absolute monarchists and other theorists critical of liberty characterize liberty as license, but not that libertarians do. He explains (correctly) why "liberty as 'absence of impediment' is an ungeneralizable norm" because "one of us can be free of impediment only by wholly dominating another" (Spragens 1992a, 33). He says that this conception of liberty is "morally unworthy," as well as "self-undermining." This conception is not a workable one, but this is why we have libertarians such as Narveson rejecting it as well.

> But this "positive" sense of the right of liberty cannot be fundamental. For positive rights entail positive duties, and positive duties of justice mean that you may be forced to do something you don't, even on due consideration, want to do . . . that is an interference with your liberty. (Spragens 1992a, 59)

Spragens's third major point is the familiar charge that the libertarian emphasis on political freedom is either based on or promotes moral relativism. As was the case in the previous argument, this too is a straw man with no textual basis in libertarian thought. (It is an interesting strategy for a non-libertarian liberal to use against libertarianism, though, because this charge is often made against all of liberalism by socialist and communitarian theorists.) The distortion is not hard to find. A libertarian might argue that the state has no business dictating moral standards because in the real world no ruler is in a better position than a citizen to know the Form of Justice. This becomes the straw man argument that society must tolerate everything because morals are subjective. But valuing political freedom is an example of demarcating the difference between right and wrong, that is, holding it wrong to coerce people into serving others' ends. It is not an example of having 'no view' about right and wrong. Libertarianism does not imply moral relativism or nihilism. Placing primary emphasis in the political realm on the autonomy of the individual does not imply a moral disconnectedness or nastiness. Quite the opposite, in fact, according to Stephen Holmes, who notes that "individualism can involve a heightened concern *for others* as individuals, rather than as faceless members of ascriptive groups" (Holmes 1988, 26).

Spragens quotes Mill as saying that a free government can survive only if people actively co-operate with the law. But that is exactly why Mill recommends the libertarian legal principle that "the sole end for which mankind are warranted, individually or collectively, in interfering with the liberty of action of any of their number is self-protection" (Mill 1859, 68). When society makes into law the wishes of the few, or even of the many, there is bound to be unrest. Mill recognized that we could all more readily agree to endorse laws prohibiting harm to others. Spragens says that "functioning civil society requires some minimum of orderliness and adherence to basic norms of behavior that distinguish it from a state of war" (Spragens 1992a, 37). That is true, but libertarian principles will satisfy this condition. Spragens here is criticizing licentiousness, not libertarianism.

When Spragens sums up this portion of his critique, he phrases it this way: "libertarian theory fails to 'see' the legitimate role that moral equality, fellow feeling, and obligation play in a good democratic society" (Spragens 1992b, 43). The libertarians I have studied see as much as anybody else that moral equality and fellow-feeling are important—indeed, for many of them moral equality is a reason for recognizing liberty—so let's consider next the charge that libertarians aren't living up to their obligations. Libertarians are typically quick to defend the importance of contracts, so Spragens must have in mind obligations not voluntarily contracted. And indeed he says that "each participant [in society] is in debt to all sorts of fellow citizens whom he or she has never met and cannot even name" (Spragens 1992b, 46). This claim is generated by the familiar argument that since he enjoys the benefits of society, he owes something to society. Can one have obligations that result from unasked-for benefits? This criticism is not based on caricature, but rather exhibits a difference in fundamental premises. A libertarian might argue that actual consent is the best way to determine obligation. Spragens might well want to challenge this and produce another account of obligation, although he does not do so here. This reveals a difference that might turn out to be incommensurable.

Spragens evidently will not accept the idea that individualism fosters respect for others by recognizing them *as* individuals, and that the solidarity that arises from voluntary cooperation in an enterprise is more substantial and authentic than state-enforced fellow feeling. He seems sympathetic to some of the reasons libertarians favor political freedom, but unwilling to explain why it is moral to force people to serve others' ends. He simply stipulates that it is, and then criticizes libertarianism for denying it.

Spragens is correct when he says that freedom and democracy are not the same thing. Libertarians are aware of this when they develop theories that give individual freedom priority over majority rule. It is begging the question, though, to argue from the premise that democratic regimes require abridgments of freedom to the conclusion that democratic regimes are good and libertarian ones are bad. What Spragens calls libertarian distortions of liberalism are either offshoots of a caricature (such as the conception of liberty as licentiousness) or moral premises he genuinely disagrees with (such as the priority of individual autonomy over the will of the majority).

Are these underlying disagreements an example of radical incommensurability? If there can be no dialogue between welfarist liberals and minimal-state liberals, would that imply that there can be no dialogue between libertarian anarchists and minimal-state libertarians? I think the first question can be answered no: freedom is a value for human beings. There are differences between the welfarist and the libertarian which can be posed not as insurmountable barriers, but as questions to be answered. Should the will of the majority ever override individual liberty? If so, under what conditions? On what terms should one consent to subordinate one's autonomy? An underlying disagreement does not by itself entail incommensurability. I think these questions can, in the long run, be resolved, and that this is in part the task of political philosophy. Another reason to resist seeing these different positions as radically incommensurable is the fact that few libertarian theorists were libertarian from birth. Narveson explicitly acknowledges a conversion from utilitarianism to libertarianism after reading Nozick (Narveson 1988, iv). Nozick too reports a philosophical evolution: "I found myself becoming convinced of (as they are now often called) libertarian views, due to various considerations and arguments" (Nozick 1974, ix). And this is of course my own experience as well. Clearly, there *is* common ground enough for some rational persuasion to take place.[29]

The answer to the second question, can there, given libertarian premises, be resolution between minimal-state libertarians and libertarian anarchists, is, I think, clearly yes, because there are no fundamental premises or values that separate anarchists from libertarian minimal-statists. As we have seen, libertarian statists and libertarian anarchists agree on the following:

1. **the nature of the state as coercive structure;**

2. **the manner in which coercion interferes with individual liberty and autonomy;**

---

29. For more on this issue, See Skoble 2008.

3. the importance of individual liberty and autonomy and their priority in the political realm.

Indeed, the anarchist criticism of minimal-state libertarianism is *generated* by this shared conception of the basic concepts. The separation occurs because the minimal-state libertarians have a particular concern about the *results* of the (otherwise desirable) lack of political authority, which I have been referring to as a "Hobbesian Fear," namely that the minimal cooperation necessary to the existence of society requires centralized political authority to come about. The polycentric-law anarchists have an answer to this concern that is consistent with the underlying shared premises, namely that cooperation of this sort can be reasonably expected to emerge in sufficient quantity to facilitate social life without political coercion. Axelrod's findings on the evolution of cooperation do not 'prove' that cooperation always or necessarily emerges spontaneously in social situations. They do, however, show that it is *possible* for cooperation to emerge spontaneously among the self-interested, without coercion from an external authority such as a political structure. If that is so, then the game theory work can be used to render more plausible the anarchists' claims about the feasibility of the social arrangements they propose. If these arrangements are feasible, the anarchists have a defensible response to the concerns of the minimal-state theorists.

What then shall we say about the problem of labels and connotations mentioned in Chapter 1? It seems to me that even if my arguments are entirely sound, it doesn't help matters to use the word 'anarchist'. One can explain the etymology, and write lengthy explanations differentiating polycentric legal systems from anarcho-syndicalism or anti-globalization hooliganism or violent, nihilistic bomb-throwing, but the history of the word will always interfere with productive discussion. (A similar problem attaches to the word 'liberal' itself: should we take that to the modern welfare state, or to the classical liberalism otherwise known as libertarianism.) Proponents of a polycentric legal order might do better to drop the 'A-word' and adopt one of two strategies, either of which would be much more conducive to productive discussion.

One would be to coin a neologism, such as 'polycentrist' or 'common-law liberal', and then elaborate as the conversation allows. Another would be to drop back to earlier labels such as 'libertarian' or 'classical liberal', and, again, elaborate as conversation develops. Labels are not, for the most part, very useful in philosophical discussion, but sometimes they are unavoidable, and in those cases, it hardly seems worth it to use one which hinders, rather than facilitates, the conversation.

Postscript: On Bomb-Throwing

Some people will continue to associate anarchism, either with or without that word, with bomb-throwing. High-school students continue to learn that President McKinley was assassinated by an anarchist. I now face two sorts of opposition: from those who are afraid that I will advocate violence against the state, and from those who are afraid I won't!

Say for the sake of argument that the state is illegitimate, that it is true that all states violate rights and hence lack true authority. Would it follow that violent action against the state would be justified? I suspect the answer is no, for the following reasons. For better or worse, the state exists, and most people regard it as legitimate, whether or not that's philosophically coherent. So a small-scale act of destruction such as killing a judge or blowing up a federal building would be perceived only as a nihilistic and destructive act, one which itself lacked moral legitimacy. And since such acts would likely harm people who are not active participants in the state's coercion, those acts *would* lack moral legitimacy. (For example, the Murrah Federal Building in Oklahoma City housed a day-care center as well as the usual assortment of bureaucrats, and in any event was not a vital command post for totalitarian coercion. Hence, although of some symbolic value for McVeigh, this was not a morally correct choice for a target.) On the other hand, what of large-scale acts of violence against the government? Say we took a page from contemporary thrillers and managed to destroy the Capitol Building while the entire legislature and executive branch was inside. That would not mean the end of government at all.

People would for the most part consider the state to still exist and have legitimacy, and would call for all the vacated positions to be filled. Put more theoretically, destroying the *current members* of the government would not destroy the *idea* of government. The vacuum would be filled immediately, and no one's mind would be changed about the ideas of spontaneous order and social rules, or the relationship between liberty and human flourishing, or the coercive nature of government. Anarchism on a libertarian model is only possible when people's *ideas* about freedom and the state change, and this cannot be accomplished by violent means, only by philosophical means. On my view, violent means could be justified in the context of a brutally repressive totalitarian state, such as that portrayed in Alan Moore and David Lloyd's graphic novel *V for Vendetta*, but not in a nominally liberal democracy. Deleting the state means something more effective than violence: it means deciding the state is not necessary. It means deleting the notion that we have no choice but to submit. The point is to peacefully change people's minds by reasoned argument, and ultimately to create the conditions in which they can flourish, not to kill them. So my philosophical defense of anarchism is not violent and doesn't entail violence, but rather implies evolutionary change in attitudes and institutions.

So if it is *not* justified to take violent action against the government, the other side wonders, what is the point? What is the 'payoff' of a theory in which government is illegitimate? It is to undermine the idea that coercion is *necessary* for social order, or that it is beneficial to human society. It is to point the way towards the continual need to scale back the scope of state power. It is to affirm the priority of liberty and its necessary connection to human flourishing, and keep us mindful of the ways in which the state, and our often unthinking obedience to it, hinders that flourishing.

Bibliography

Anderson, Terry, and P.J. Hill. 1979. An American Experiment in Anarcho-Capitalism. *Journal of Libertarian Studies* 3:1.

———. 2004. *The Not So Wild Wild West: Property Rights on the Frontier.* Stanford Economics and Finance.

Aquinas, Thomas. 1988. *Summa Theolgiae*, Question 91. In Paul E. Sigmund, ed., *St. Thomas Aquinas on Politics and Ethics* (New York: Norton).

Aristotle. 1999. *Nicomachean Ethics.* Translated by T. Irwin. Indianapolis: Hackett.

Arnold, N. Scott. 2002. The Role of Government in Responding to Natural Catastrophes. In Machan 2002.

Axelrod, Robert. 1984. *The Evolution of Cooperation.* New York: Basic Books.

Axelrod, Robert, and William D. Hamilton. 1981. The Evolution of Cooperation. *Science* 211, 1390–96.

Bakunin, Mikhail. 1990. *Statism and Anarchy.* Translated by Marshall Shatz. Cambridge: Cambridge University Press.

Barnett, Randy E. 1985. Pursuing Justice in a Free Society: Part One—Power vs. Liberty. *Criminal Justice Ethics* (Summer–Fall).

———. 1986. Pursuing Justice in a Free Society: Part Two—Crime Prevention and the Legal Order. *Criminal Justice Ethics* (Winter–Spring).

———. 1998. *The Structure of Liberty: Justice and the Rule of Law.* Oxford: Oxford University Press.

Bastiat, Frédéric. 1987 [1850]. *The Law.* Irvington-on-Hudson: Foundation for Economic Education.

Beito, David T. 2000. *From Mutual Aid to the Welfare State: Fraternal Societies and Social Services, 1890–1967.* University of North Carolina Press.

Berman, Harold. 1983. *Law and Revolution.* Cambridge, Massachusetts: Harvard University Press.

Benson, Bruce L. 1990. *The Enterprise of Law: Justice Without the State.* San Francisco: Pacific Research Institute.

Berlin, Isaiah. 1967 [1958]. Two Concepts of Liberty. In Quinton 1967.

Coleman, Jules L. 1988. Rights, Markets, and Community. *Harvard Journal of Law and Public Policy* 11:3 (Summer).

―――. 1992. *Risks and Wrongs.* Cambridge: Cambridge University Press.

Depew, David, and Bruce Weber, eds. 1985. *Evolution at a Crossroads.* Cambridge, Massachusetts: MIT Press.

Dyke, C. 1985. Complexity and Closure. In DePew and Weber 1985.

Elster, Jon. 1982. Sour Grapes. In Sen and Williams 1982.

Freeman, Samuel. 2001. The Illiberalism of Libertarianism. *Philosophy and Public Affairs* (Spring).

Friedman, David. 1989. *The Machinery of Freedom: Guide to a Radical Capitalism.* Second edition. La Salle: Open Court.

Gauthier, David. 1986. *Morals by Agreement.* Oxford: Clarendon.

Hamowy, Ronald. 1978. Law and the Liberal Society. *Journal of Libertarian Studies* 2:4.

Hampton, Jean. 1986. *Hobbes and the Social Contract Tradition.* Cambridge: Cambridge University Press.

Hart, H.L.A. 1961. *The Concept of Law.* Oxford: Clarendon.

Hayek, Friedrich A. 1960. *The Constitution of Liberty.* Chicago: University of Chicago Press.

―――. 1973. *Law, Legislation, and Liberty.* Three volumes. Chicago: University of Chicago Press.

Hobbes, Thomas. 1951 [1651]. *Leviathan.* New York: Penguin.

Hogue, Arthur R. 1966. *Origins of the Common Law.* Indianapolis: Liberty Press.

Holmes, Stephen. 1988. The Community Trap. *The New Republic* (28th November).

Hume, David. 1948 [1777]. Of the Original Contract. In Hume, *Moral and Political Philosophy.* (New York: Hafner).

Kavka, Gregory. 1986. *Hobbesian Moral and Political Theory.* Princeton: Princeton University Press.

Lavoie, Don. 1993. Democracy, Markets, and the Legal Order: Notes on the Nature of Politics in a Radically Liberal Society. *Social Philosophy and Policy* 10:2 (Summer).

Lester, J.C. 2000. *Escape from Leviathan: Liberty, Welfare, and Anarchy Reconciled.* New York: St. Martin's Press.

Locke, John. 1967 [1690]. *Two Treatises of Government.* Cambridge: Cambridge University Press.

Luce, R.Duncan, and Howard Raiffa. 1957. *Games and Decisions: Introduction and Critical Survey*. New York: Wiley.

Luntley, Michael. 1989. *The Meaning of Socialism*. La Salle: Open Court.

Machan, Tibor. 1975. *Human Rights and Human Liberties*. Chicago: Nelson-Hall, 1975.

———, ed. 1982. *The Libertarian Reader*. Totowa: Rowman and Littlefield.

———. 1983. Individualism and the Problem of Political Authority. *The Monist* 63:4 (October).

———. 1989. *Individuals and Their Rights*. La Salle: Open Court.

———, ed. 2002. *Liberty and Hard Cases*. Hoover Institution Press.

Marx, Karl. 1977. *Selected Writings*. Edited by David McLellan. Oxford: Oxford University Press.

Mill, John Stuart. 1985 [1859]. *On Liberty*. New York: Penguin.

Moore, Alan, and David Lloyd. 1988. *V for Vendetta*. DC/Warner.

Moss, David A. 1999. Courting Disaster? The Transformation of Federal Disaster Policy Since 1803. In Kenneth A. Froot, ed., *The Financing of Catastrophe Risk* (Chicago: University of Chicago Press).

Murray, Charles. 1984. *Losing Ground*. New York: Basic Books.

Narveson, Jan. 1988. *The Libertarian Idea*. Philadelphia: Temple University Press.

Nozick, Robert. 1974. *Anarchy, State, and Utopia*. New York: Basic Books.

———. 1993. *The Nature of Rationality*. Princeton: Princeton University Press.

———. 2003. *Invariances*. Cambridge, Massachusetts: Belknap Press.

Nowak, Martin, and Karl Sigmund. 1993. A Strategy of Win-Stay, Lose-Shift that Outperforms Tit-for-Tat in the Prisoner's Dilemma Game. *Nature* 364 (1st July).

Oliver, Daniel T. 1999. Helping the Needy: Lessons from the Chicago Fire. *Capital Research Center Newsletter* (July).

Olson, Mancur. 1965. *The Logic of Collective Action: Public Goods and the Theory of Groups*. Cambridge, Massachusetts: Harvard University Press.

Plato. 1997. *Complete Works*. Edited by John Cooper. Indianapolis: Hackett.

Proudhon, Pierre-Joseph. 1964. What Is Property? In Albert Fried and Ronald Sanders, eds., *Socialist Thought* (New York: Doubleday).

Quinton, Anthony, ed. 1967. *Political Philosophy*. Oxford: Oxford University Press.

Rasmussen, Douglas B. 1982. Essentialism, Values, and Rights: The Objectivist Case for the Free Society. In Machan 1982.

———. 1999. Human Flourishing and the Appeal to Human Nature. *Social Philosophy and Policy* 16:1 (Winter).

Rasmussen, Douglas B., and Douglas J. Den Uyl. 1991. *Liberty and Nature: An Aristotelian Defense of Liberal Order.* La Salle: Open Court.

———. 2005. *Norms of Liberty: A Perfectionist Basis for Non-Perfectionist Politics.* University Park: Pennsylvania State University Press.

Rawls, John. 1971. *A Theory of Justice.* Cambridge, Massachusetts: Harvard University Press.

Rothbard, Murray N. 1970. *Power and Market: Government and the Economy.* Menlo Park: Institute for Humane Studies.

———. 1973. *For a New Liberty.* New York: Macmillan.

———. 1978. Society Without a State. *Nomos* 19.

Sen, Amartya, and Bernard Williams, eds. 1982. *Utilitarianism and Beyond.* Cambridge: Cambridge University Press.

Schmidtz, David. 1991. *The Limits of Government: An Essay on the Public Goods Argument.* Boulder: Westview.

Shirer, William. 1959. *The Rise and Fall of the Third Reich.* New York: Simon and Schuster.

Skoble, Aeon James. 1991. Conflicting Visions of Liberalism. *Dialogue* 33 (April).

———. 1992. Another Caricature of Libertarianism. *Reason Papers* 17 (Fall).

———. 2002. Liberty, Policy, and Natural Disasters. In Machan 2002.

———. 2008. *Reading Rasmussen and Den Uyl: Critical Essays on Norms of Liberty.* Lanham: Lexington Books.

Spragens, Thomas. 1992a. The Limitations of Libertarianism, Part 1. *The Responsive Community* 2:1 (Winter).

———. 1992b. The Limitations of Libertarianism, Part 2. *The Responsive Community* 2:2 (Spring).

Steiner, Hillel. 1977. The Structure of a Set of Compossible Rights. *Journal of Philosophy* 74.

Stringham, Edward, ed. 2007. *Anarchy and the Law.* Oakland: Independent Institute.

Taylor, Michael. 1987. *The Possibility of Cooperation.* Cambridge: Cambridge University Press.

Wolff, Robert Paul. 1970. *In Defense of Anarchism.* New York: Harper Torchbooks.

Index

125